FUGITIVES

To order additional copies of
FUGITIVES,
by
William E. Richardson,
call
1-800-765-6955.

Visit us at
www.reviewandherald.com
for information on other Review and Herald® products.

William E.
Richardson

God's Relentless Pursuit of His Beloved

FUGITIVES

REVIEW AND HERALD® PUBLISHING ASSOCIATION
HAGERSTOWN, MD 21740

The author assumes full responsibility for the accuracy of all facts and quotations as cited in this book.

This book was
Edited by Patricia J. Fritz
Copyedited by James Cavil
Cover designed by Trent Truman
Cover photo by Comstock Images
Interior designed by Candy Harvey
Electronic makeup by Tina Ivany
Typeset: 11.5/13.5 Bembo

PRINTED IN U.S.A.

08 07 06 05 5 4 3 2 1

R&H Cataloging Service
Richardson, William Edwin, 1937-
Fugitives.

1. Bible—Biography I. Title.

220.92

ISBN 0-8280-1830-8

DEDICATION

To my three children,
Cindy, Cheri, and Steve,
and their spouses,
Roy Schmidt, Ken Leffler, and Andrea (Cielsielski) Richardson.

Their quick and inquiring minds have consistently challenged me
to present the truths of Scripture
in a way that is both clear and interesting.

In these stories of famous biblical fugitives,
I believe these goals have been achieved.

CONTENTS

INTRODUCTION

FOR MOST CHRISTIANS the walk of faith is more like climbing Mount Everest than strolling through the garden. We are told that Enoch walked with God, and it sounds so peaceful and pastoral and easy. But when we're caught up in the pace of today, that placid walk with God seems elusive indeed. We balance work schedules so that at least one parent is available when the kids are not in school or day care. We rush home from work by way of the grocery store and frenetically work our way through the dinner hour. Afterward we hope there is enough sunlight left to mow some lawn or finish two other odd jobs. Then, after dark, we should pay some bills; but it's so hard to keep the checkbook balanced, and it's more relaxing to watch TV, in which position we fall asleep. Enoch, with his pastoral life and light schedule, had it easy. Even I could have walked with God back then. But busyness is here to stay—we just can't live in another time or place. In the Western world of today there is no cure for the common cold or the overburdened schedule. Still, though it's never enough, we usually manage to crowd in a little God time in the mornings and on weekends, and our faith lurches on.

But for many of us the walk of faith is plagued by a more fundamental problem than busyness: faith itself keeps getting tested. Some can justly sing, "I've wandered far away from God, now I'm coming home; the paths of sin too long I've trod; Lord, I'm coming home." But that doesn't seem to apply to large numbers of us struggling Christians. In all honesty, it's been a while since we wandered far away from God. We haven't knowingly gone exploring on the paths of sin.

Rather, while we were making some progress right on the path of faith, doubt and uncertainty seemed to leap up out of nowhere. Once it was an unspeakable tragedy of death. A close friend lost three small children. Faith winced. Another time it was the lingering agony of Alzheimer's that slowly dragged to an end the life of a faithful tithepayer. Faith staggered. Later it was the coldly calculating, self-serving action of some high church official. Cynicism sprang to life.

Years ago when the love interests of my siblings and me were waxing and waning, our dad was fond of "comforting" us with the unhelpful bromide "The path of love is very rocky." A slight change of metaphor may help us here. The path of faith is never far from the thickets of doubt and uncertainty. Admittedly the path is not a broad one, so the briars of cynicism can sometimes snag us. And before we are hardly aware, we have wandered off into the brambles of discontent and disillusionment, where we may wander for days. At times the detour is nasty, and we end up scratched and scarred. Other times it feels rewarding to be insightful and not gullible, and we would just as soon not return to the path of simple faith. But however we feel at the time in our inmost souls, we know that it is only the path of faith that will lead us to our real destination.

Bearing in mind the many distractions and our tendency, once off the path of faith, to get more and more entangled in thickets of doubt, I found great encouragement in the following verse from Francis Thompson's "The Hound of Heaven."

"I fled Him, down the nights and down the days;
I fled Him, down the arches of the years;
I fled Him, down the labyrinthine ways
Of my own mind; and in the mist of tears
I hid from Him, and under running laughter.
Up vistaed hopes I sped;
And shot, precipitated,
Adown Titanic glooms of chasmèd fears,

From those strong Feet that followed, followed after.

But with unhurrying chase,

And unperturbèd pace,

Deliberate speed, majestic instancy,

They beat—and a Voice beat

More instant than the Feet—

'All things betray thee, who betrayest Me.' "*

It is a gripping figure that speaks of the human proclivity not simply to wander from God, but to try actively to flee from Him. And such running from God has a very long history. It started with Adam and Eve and, in varying degrees, has characterized the lives of the great and the not-so-great. In fact, fugitives from God come in a mind-boggling array of shapes and circumstances. Some of the most famous biblical heroes were fugitives first. Furthermore, it is often from their experience of running that we learn our most powerful lessons.

The figure of fleeing may seem too strong for many Christians who feel they are really trying to understand and follow God's lead. But since the best of biblical characters had times of flight (as we shall see in the chapters that follow), should we pretend that it doesn't happen to us? Isn't it true that the inexplicable, maddening unfairness in the world, the political maneuvering in the church, the seemingly unanswered prayers, have all, on occasion, driven us into thickets of doubt and cynicism? Sooner or later we all take on, even if briefly, the role of fugitive from God. The good word is that the brambles are never so thick or the distance from the path so great that the Hound of Heaven can't find us.

Of course, most analogies are flawed at some point, and this one is no exception. In fact, at first thought it doesn't even seem appropriate. The biblical view of dogs was anything but complimentary. The animal was usually presented as a figure of uncleanness and revulsion. But historically the hound symbolizes a tenacious hunter and tracker that far exceeds humans in finding its prey. It is that one canine trait that this book seeks to emphasize. Still, the best face we can put on the dog figure is so far removed from the meaning and sense of God that any comparison may seem to many like an enormous sacrilege. At the same time, a symbol with a serious discontinuity can be a gripping figure that rivets the mind on an important truth.

So this collection of essays makes no attempt to portray the many faces and traits of God. Instead, this is a series of glimpses at God's relentless pursuit of His runaway children. Like a tracking hound, He cannot rest until He has found every lost child. But then what? While He is strong enough to drag each one back to the path from which we have strayed, He restrains that instinct of rescue. Since free will got us lost, free will must remain at the heart of the rescue. His sudden presence by our brambles of doubt or anger does not, of itself, save us; but it is a dramatic reminder of our hopelessness, and hints that if we choose to follow, He will lead us to safety. And one of the surprises is His patience when we linger in our lost-ness, or choose to get lost more than once or twice. Human rescuers and regular hounds have little patience for that sort of thing; the Hound of Heaven is different. He is urgent but not impatient, insistent but not coercive. It is truly amazing to watch Him work.

---

*In Francis P. LeBuffe, *The Hound of Heaven, An Interpretation* (New York: MacMillan Co., 1921), p. 19.

CHAPTER 1

ADAM AND EVE:
The First Fugitives

As WE STROLLED THROUGH Yosemite Valley, moonlight caressing the mammoth rock walls and turning the Merced River into a silver ribbon, my wife and I wondered if Eden could have been more beautiful. Shortly thereafter we arrived back at our campsite just after the bear had gone through. No one was hurt, but there were a few moments of fear, and our ice chest carries scars to this day. Then the mosquitoes came. Much later, the headline: "Yosemite rock climber killed in fall." When we take the time to notice, beauty spots are everywhere. Pick your favorite. Not far removed, and often right in the middle, is a nettle or a gnat or poison ivy or a bear. Utopia it is not.

Back in the sixteenth century, as he pondered all the beauty of this world, Sir Thomas More wrote a work called *Utopia,* in which he presented an idealistic society with beautiful solutions to all the usual social problems. He wrote in glowing terms of this unusual island where all was peace and the few laws were faithfully kept. More asserted that the Utopians had successfully plucked pride from their hearts. The seeds of ambition and friction were absent, so there was no competitive strife. There, the greatest pleasures were those of the mind, and the people were tireless in intellectual pursuits.

Some reviewers looked upon More's work as merely a protracted joke. Others have felt that if he meant it as a joke, it turned out to be a cruel joke, as many people took it quite seriously as a goal toward which society should strive. Also, coming as it did only 25 years after the discovery of America, some saw in it an idealistic portrayal of the New World. I view it as expressing a kind of yearning for that paradise long lost that we were meant for, a paradise we see but dimly reflected in all the beauty spots of earth.

On Planet Earth today the beauty is often missed because of all the ugliness and carnage. In the natural world volcanoes blow the tops off pristine mountains, and killer earthquakes shake down buildings and freeways and crush out the lives of hapless hundreds. Nature as well as human life can turn so quickly from beauty to ugliness and bestiality. That beautiful baby asleep in mother's arms may soon be neglected or even brutalized for crying too much. A handful of humans, twisted in mind and heart, bring vicious new meaning to the word *terrorist,* and thousands of innocents die in minutes.

In such a time, thinking humans wonder how a world with so many hints of paradise could come to such a state. One thing is clear: it couldn't have been through evolution. The theory that the passing eons have brought higher life forms with improved moral awareness has been turned on its head. The lower life forms were never as debased and malicious as humans have become. A more reasonable explanation of today's world is the biblical one. It portrays a perfect start with an entire world of Yosemite Valleys. Then the devil and sin gained a toehold, and the inexorable slide toward hell began.

But let's look at that picture of perfection we refer to as Eden. A clearer grasp of how things began may help us better understand some of the questions that vex us today. If humans were in fact designed and built by a great Creator, then the description of their creation and the circumstances of their first surroundings can tell us a lot about what God intended and what would contribute to the success of the first family and following generations. Any manufactured product, especially one with moving parts, should come with an owner's manual or at least some suggestions about how the product can operate most successfully.

Scene one was big on natural environment: "The earth brought forth vegetation: plants . . . , and trees of every kind bearing fruit" (Gen. 1:12, NRSV). In that setting, creatures of every size and shape grazed and scampered, and swarms of life inhabited the seas and skies. Peace reigned, and apparently there was no preying on one another for food. "See, I have given you every plant yielding seed . . . and every tree with seed in its fruit;

you shall have them for food. And to every beast of the earth, and to every bird of the air, and to everything that creeps on the earth, everything that has the breath of life, I have given every green plant for food" (verses 29, 30, NRSV). Were the lions' teeth square? Did lions have claws? Were fleas a later mutation? Many questions remain, but if faith in a benevolent Creator is the given, it is not hard to imagine that "all was perfect, worthy of its divine Author" (Ellen G. White, *Patriarchs and Prophets,* p. 47).

Then, in the east, God planted a garden, and in the midst of it all He made Adam and Eve, beautiful and flawless, but not perfect. Well, at least not perfect in the sense that they had no room to improve.

Absolute perfection, a state beyond the grasp of sinful minds, implies that there is nothing unknown, unlearned, unexperienced. But Adam and Eve had so much to learn that the term *perfection* would apply only to their physique and to their potential, not to their moral and mental development. For created beings with free will, moral and spiritual maturity is demonstrated and developed only through testing and trial. These two magnificent creatures were set apart from all the others when God said, "Let us make man in our image, after our likeness" (verse 26, RSV). It was a wonderful and mysterious difference from all the rest of creation. Whatever it meant to be in God's image, it enabled humans to commune with and have some level of fellowship with God. Above all, it included "individuality, power to think and to do" (Ellen G. White, *Education,* p. 17). And that meant making choices, which brings us back to the matter of testing and maturity and loyalty.

Somewhere in that garden were two trees. The tree of life had something to do with providing physical vitality; and, as important as that is, it doesn't get much attention in the written record. It's the other tree that gets all the interest, in large part because it was off-limits. What is there about forbidden fruit that makes it the most attractive? Perhaps it has something to do with the kind of creative, inquisitive minds the Creator gave us. Surely there is a great deal summed up in that descriptive phrase "power to think and to do." Adam and Eve were thinkers. They were also made to have fellowship with God. Now, that word *fellowship* can describe many different kinds of relationships. It can refer to mere social interaction, such as between members of the country club or schoolmates or even gorillas. Fellowship is greatly enriched, however, when it includes the deeper elements of love and trust and belief in. But the moment those elements become present, we assume a certain level of thinking and testing.

To put it very simply, Adam and Eve's trust in and loyalty to God had to be tested. Trust in a person would be hard to verify if there were never any opportunities to demonstrate that trust. Similarly, the concept of loyalty makes the most sense when there is at least the possibility of disloyalty. And even love, while it need not be exclusive to only one other person, is most intense when its focus narrows from many options to just one. All of which suggests that for Adam and Eve to be called loyal and trustworthy, they first needed to be confronted by options/tests; hence, the forbidden tree. For Adam and Eve the first test was not a matter of choosing between their Maker or the devil. The Creator didn't need a devil to construct a test. All that was needed was for humans to be given the power of reasoning and then be confronted with the possibility of trust and acceptance on the one hand, and doubt and disbelief on the other.

Of course, the evil one quickly got involved in the process, but all he had to do was help them focus on their own importance as thinkers and individuals. His slickly worded temptation didn't focus on himself. Everything about the temptation focused on the humans as thinkers and doers—those very qualities that made them most like God Himself. To narrow the focus of the first temptation to appetite is to miss the entire thrust of the test. The real heart of the temptation was in that little phrase "You will be like God" (Gen. 3:5, RSV). It obviously helped the temptation along to dazzle Eve with a talking serpent and some beautiful fruit, but that was primarily for purpose of distraction. The real issue was whether to follow God or her own reason. She hadn't known Him very long, so the development of trust was still in the early stages. Of course, the talking serpent was an even more recent acquaintance, so she had even less reason to believe its word. As she pondered God's restriction and her own ability as a thinker, the desire to be "like God" and exercise her individuality won out. Adam concurred. They both stepped away from God.

You would think that a God-imaged life—a life of rational thought and reflection, in which all mental, physical, and spiritual needs were met—would be adequate and completely satisfying. But that is to underestimate the inquisitiveness and vigor of thought in those first humans. They obviously felt the need to think things through for themselves and then experience as much of life as possible. Accordingly, the suggestion that they could be "like God" sounded too exciting to pass up. But since they were already in His image, how would it be different to be like Him? In his book *King Jesus' Manual of Arms for the 'Armless* (Nashville: Abingdon Press, 1973) Vernard Eller suggests the analogy of the ballerina and the lead dancer. As long as the ballerina (the first humans) follows closely the steps and movements of her lead dancer, all is in perfect synchronization, and there is harmony and beauty of movement. But if the ballerina should suddenly attempt to step into the role of lead dancer and be a second lead, there would be confusion, and anything but harmony and synchronization would result (p. 22).

The beautiful thing about the ballerina's movements is that they are truly her movements. While she follows her lead through the choreography, her graceful leaps and moves are still hers. What makes them so impressive and beautiful is that they are in perfect synchronization with her lead; yet, at the same time, they are truly her movements. She is not a puppet. What an awful thing it would be if the ballerina were tied to her lead. Her movements, then, would be perfectly synchronized; she would do everything just right, but they wouldn't really be her movements. Often people pray that God will lead them, and they frequently have in mind this kind of leading. They talk as if it would be just great with them if God made all the moves for them. But free will just doesn't come that cheap. Free will means that after we pray for guidance, we must then think hard and weigh evidences. It is often a difficult process, but God knows it will lead us to a more mature, developed relationship with Him than would be possible for a puppet. God doesn't really have much use for puppets on a string.

So Adam and Eve tried to advance from lowly images of God to being just like Him. As soon as they made that attempt, everything began to fall apart. Whatever their expectations, all kinds of surprises hit them. In the place of peace and harmony, hostility and accusation sprang up. "The woman whom you gave to be with me, she gave me fruit from the tree, and I ate" (verse 12, NRSV). Just 15 verses earlier she was "bone of my bone, flesh of my flesh, the one with whom I have become one" (see Gen. 2:23). What a difference a sin makes! Whereas before, she was his very inspiration, now she has become "that woman *You* foisted on me. Lord, I'm not to blame; *You* created her." And Eve continued the whimpering. "The serpent tricked me, and I ate" (Gen. 3:13, NRSV). The attitude of finding someone to blame for our failures has a very long and stubborn history.

Another sudden and unexpected change was their sense of shame at their nakedness. They had been naked all along, but without shame (Gen. 2:25). What kind of nudity was it that was innocent and shameless? We can only speculate, but perhaps that original nakedness represented such things as openness, honesty, or even love and acceptance. Perhaps it also indicated adequacy to be in God's presence with no covering, that in the presence of God all covering is superficial and inadequate. Much less important, it also hints at a mild climate, rather smooth ground cover for walking, and no predatory insects in the air or in the grass.

The catastrophic consequences of their self-serving act would come upon them only a little at a time. Never would they be able to grasp its full enormity. No human could survive such a revelation. For now, this first chill of nakedness was enough to mystify and frighten them. Had the consequences not been so tragic, their sudden search for large leaves and viney thread would have been almost humorous. With its subtropical climate Eden probably grew something like elephant ear plants with huge tough leaves. At least we can hope that they had more to work with than willow or maple leaves.

Whatever covering they came up with didn't do the job: when the Lord approached, they felt as naked as ever. Why was that? What was it about their simple act that made them feel so . . . well, so uncovered before their Maker, even when they were thoroughly wrapped in leaves? The huge importance of putting self-interest before God, later to become known as sin, would never be understood by Adam and Eve or by any of their children. Furthermore, the fallacy that the resulting nakedness might be covered by natural materials and human hustle is so stubborn that every person has tried it. But Adam and Eve's experiences should have taught us the futility of any such human effort.

Those new sensations of vulnerability and fear drove them to try two impossibilities. First, they tried to cover themselves adequately; then, they tried to hide from God. But the Hound of Heaven could track them unerringly. They quickly learned that that hidden corner of the garden and those ridiculous leaves provided absolutely no cover from the eyes of God.

I can hear that pitiful exchange as the Lord approached them. "Wait over there, Lord; we aren't quite decent. Give us just a few minutes, and we'll be much better covered; these leaves are really hard to manage."

To which He might have said, "Sure, I'll wait. I'm in no hurry. Take as long as you want. It's important to feel presentable and prepared. I'll just wait over here until you make yourselves ready. Just let Me know when you feel that you've done enough."

How long would He have had to wait? How much effort would it have taken? How many layers of leaves would have been enough? But that scenario never happened. What actually happened almost defies belief. Genesis 3:21 presents us with the most impressive scene of the entire Garden of Eden story: "And the Lord God made for Adam and for his wife garments of skins, and clothed them" (RSV). What an incredible story. God created humans in perfect innocence, surrounded them with a beautiful garden, and made sure every possible need was met. He gave them a power of reason somehow like His own, and confronted them with realistic options that would require choices with consequences. On the one hand, as they responded to Him and followed His lead, their understanding would continually increase as they grew in harmony with His will. The result would be continuous peace and contentment. On the other hand, if they chose to follow their own instincts and desires, a dire threat reverberated in the chambers of their minds: "You shall die."

Whereupon, they chose option two. "We don't want just to follow God's lead and stay in His image and dance His dance. We want to be *like* Him and also to be individuals and dance our own dance and take some steps we can call our own." And when they, knowing the consequences, made their decision, it appeared that the serpent's suggestion was right: they didn't die. Nevertheless, something awesome and terrible had begun. They didn't know what it all meant; they knew only that they were suddenly naked and totally inadequate.

So the loving Creator who had not been believed or trusted, who had been told He wasn't really needed, stooped very low, killed some of His innocent animals, fashioned clothes from their skins, and draped those pitiful and frightened nudes. The first powerful display of grace involved the shedding of blood to cover the results of sin. As they stood helpless, exposed, and totally unpresentable, nothing they could do would resolve their dilemma. And that is always the context of grace. Grace is love and compassion, doing something for humans that they cannot possibly do for themselves. The trembling, unworthy, self-serving couple must have watched, dumbstruck, as their Creator stooped and bloodied His own hands to fashion a covering they were never supposed to need.

One additional reflection on this picture is helpful. As God considered their deed, He was confronted by only a few options. He could just overlook their self-serving act. After all, it was a first offense, and maybe He could explain to them how important it would be never to do such a thing again. That would have been merciful, but it would have belittled the seriousness of His earlier word of warning. That course of action would have shown mercy but not justice. Or He might have said, "The divine warning was clear enough. There is nothing more I could have done or said. Their guilt is real, and their sentence cannot be changed. They will have to die."

But there was a third option that could be conceived only in the mind of God. Only the divine mind could fashion a plan that would perfectly combine justice and mercy in the same act. He had earlier given that awesome warning, "In the day that you eat of [the tree] you shall die" (Gen. 2:17, NRSV). That word of God was not idle chatter, like so much human hot air. It was a statement of the inexorable consequences of stepping away from God's will. But by an unfathomable process of substitution, He allowed the death of innocent animals to cover the wretchedness of guilty humans. In this way He combined death and life in one incredible act. Who but a loving God could have imagined such a union of justice and mercy? No doubt it took years for the importance and symbolism of that act to register on human minds.

That act of mercy—and that symbol of future salvation—was a powerful magnet, designed to keep attracting humans back to the track from which they had strayed. At the same time a terrible choice had been made, and the consequences had to follow. The promise that disobedience would bring death would be worked out in a million horrible ways. Of course, they didn't die that day; but, in addition to the animals that died, there was a larger kind of death that set in. For that day was the beginning of every human depravity and death. It is not too strong to say that the beginning of sin was the beginning of death.

Or to put it another way, that day of disobedience was the beginning of the death/life that has characterized our world from that time to this. If there can be any explanation of the agonies of our present world, it must come from this warning at the very beginning. Often when we cry out against the seeming unfairness of God, we do so in isolation from His early warning about the long-range impact of sin. If we try to understand the meaning of leukemia in a 9-year-old, apart from this idea that sin brought about a death/life on this planet, we will never succeed. If we are filled only with angry "whys" about the atrocities and inequities of this life, it is because we have not yet listened carefully to God's early warning about the seriousness of sin and separation from His will. He tried to make it clear to our first parents: death in all its hideous forms will begin for you and all your children the day you separate yourselves from the divine plan. But, as we have seen, in spite of the warning, no sooner had they wandered off than the Hound of Heaven proceeded with His first rescue effort. "And the Lord God made . . . garments of skin, and clothed them" (Gen. 3:21, RSV). That thought should buoy us up in those frequent times when the grief of this life threatens to overwhelm our faith.

Many generations later the apostle Paul seemed to pick up on the theme of justice and mercy symbolized in Genesis 2. In Ephesians 2 he paints a despairing picture of human wretchedness and depravity. The distance between God and humanity, begun by Adam and Eve, has only increased, until humans are now "aliens from the commonwealth of Israel, . . . having no hope, and without God in the world" (Eph. 2:12)—sort of like those helpless nudes in the garden. "But now in Christ Jesus you who once were far off have been brought near by the blood of Christ" (verse 13, RSV). Like the first Adam and Eve, all the modern-day Adams and Eves have stepped away from God's leading, determined to make a go of it with their own intelligence as their only guide and god. Sooner or later a sense of inadequacy and nakedness creeps over them. Fortunately, He has never been content to leave us wandering about with only His words of warning ringing in our heads. Instead He steps back into our lives, not with the blood of innocent animals, but with His own blood, which draws us near once more. Clearly the Hound of Heaven is more than a tracking animal. He has bled for us as well.

CHAPTER 2

CAIN AND ABEL:

The Hound Tracks the Siblings

THERE IS SOMETHING ABOUT THE NAME CAIN. When I was a child, one of my father's many warnings was against "raising Cain." "When you guys get out of school early tomorrow, I don't want you hanging around, raising Cain." I wasn't exactly sure what it included, but I knew I'd better avoid doing it. I also have noticed that while there are frequent modern-day Seths and Isaacs and Adams and even an occasional Abel, I can't recall meeting a modern-day Cain. Was the name tainted by its very first use? The fact is, while Adam and Eve illustrated how the Hound of Heaven will pursue and call back those who strayed, their firstborn clearly illustrates that there are limits to His calling power. Those limits center on the importance to God of free choice and the ominous consequences of a wrong use of that power to choose. But if God's tracking and calling after His straying Adam and Eve can be called a success, then surely the story of Cain must be called a failure.

Of course, from failures we can learn some of our most indelible lessons. The morning that I, in a rush, washed my contact lens down the drain, I learned several lessons that years of successful lens cleanings had not taught me. That failure taught me not only about better handling of contact lenses, but about the construction and maintenance of sink drains, the meaning of patience, the futility of panic, and even a lesson or two about prayer. This is not to say that God sends us failures to teach us. Nor is it that there is a specific purpose to be served by each particular failure or heartache that comes our way. It is that the Lord has given us the ability to learn and grow from the failures we experience or observe. And in the Bible there are numerous failures from which we can learn.

Throughout Scripture there are personalities that seem to go into free fall from the moment they come into focus. For some, like Nadab (1 Kings 15:25, 26), there is a brief reference, then a sudden flameout explained by the phrase "he did what was evil in the sight of the Lord," and they are gone. For others, there are minute details of malicious intrigue, rebellion, murder, greed, sexual indulgence, and petty vengeance, all of which can be seen in the families of the first two kings of Israel, Saul and David. But they are included in sacred Scripture, not to titillate us or to suggest that sin and its results have a purpose. Such failures had to be included because, if a history of humans was to be written, they could not be excluded. After Adam, humans of failure were the only kind God had to work with. It should hardly surprise us that some of the failures were catastrophic and irredeemable.

But it is important that we view the sins and disasters and sorrows of the Bible properly. The Cains of Scripture don't have some kind of necessary place in God's plan. The tragedies are not designed so that we can learn from them. In other words, God didn't create a Cain to teach us the awfulness of sibling rivalry. Rather, the Bible stories show us real humans making choices of their own free will and then living out the consequences of those choices. In fact, in this story it is almost as if the decision-making process is set before us in slow motion, with God knowing ahead of time the direction of Cain's thoughts and attempting to dissuade him from the bad decision he is about to make. Genesis 4:6 and 7 give us the clearest picture of God in this story, and He is, at the same time, reasoning, inviting, pleading, and redemptive. "The Lord said to Cain, 'Why are you angry, and why has your countenance fallen? If you do well, will you not be accepted? And if you do not do well, sin is crouching at the door; its desire is for you, but you must master it'" (RSV). Here is a real person contemplating a real choice, being coached by God, not coerced by Him. Clearly the good and bad examples in Scripture show us the results of real choices by real people, not predetermined outcomes acted out by puppets dancing on strings held by God. Paul suggested that all these things were "written down to instruct us" (1 Cor. 10:11, NRSV). It is an important statement, because it says that these biblical stories were *preserved* so that we could learn from them, not that they *happened* so that we could learn from them. So Scripture is designed to give us examples of all kinds to help us see the results of decisions freely made for and against God, which hopefully influence our decisions to be for God, not against Him. The freedom of the individual has always been God's paramount concern.

Modern parents know that their children won't be perfect. After all, they are us made over again. But everything for Adam and Eve was a first; there was no history from which to learn. So just what did they expect in their children? Probably something akin to perfection, though they surely didn't know the meaning of that word. Given the abbreviated account in Scripture, any extended profile of the first children that might detail their traits and personality would be the result of considerable interpretation and a lot of creativity. Still, the biblical highlights, though few, are intriguing and suggestive.

Observations about Cain and Abel as boys are hidden in the mists of history, since Scripture leaps their lives from birth directly to young adulthood. Still, young adult behavior does not spring up full-blown in the adult years. Random acts for good or evil are rarely that. More likely, acts for good or evil are the natural outworking of the training, makeup, and complex influences that have shaped each individual life.

In the beautiful but still mysterious world around them, Adam and Eve watched the now-furtive animals begin to bear their young. It was all so amazing, so new, so beyond explaining. Some animal babies seemed totally functional and active mere moments after birth, while others seemed more dead than alive. But which was the preview of human birth? How long would it take, and just how would the birth process happen? There were no books or old wives' tales, and with the advent of sin, even God wasn't explaining things as before.

After the Garden of Eden the remorse of Adam and Eve must have been staggering. The enormity of their deed surely mushroomed as they played and replayed that scene and heard again that haunting question from the Lord, "What is this that you have done?" (Gen. 3:13, RSV). As the months passed and they observed falling leaves, dying flowers, and terrified animals, their remorse must have become sheer torment. If only they could come up with some rational explanation for their behavior, it might make their grief more manageable; but relief could not come so easily or soon.

Of the billions of human pregnancies, surely there are two that stand apart from all the others: Eve's first and Mary's first. Eve's because there had never been one, and Mary's because of its origin. As Eve's pregnancy took shape, hope grew. That mysterious pronouncement about her "seed" bruising the serpent's head (verse 15) meant that, somehow, the first child would help to solve their terrible problem; that the work of that weird serpent, reclusive, and untalkative since that first day, would be somehow undone when the first baby was born. The anticipation of the first parents-to-be knew no bounds. Surely no baby born since has been more eagerly awaited or had more expected of it. At last the excitement and anticipation burst, and the first-ever human baby was born. If after untold millions of childbirths we still experience the event with agony and awe, what emotions must this first one have aroused? They expected a Messiah, but instead they got Cain.

Of course, his birth didn't really blunt the anticipation or resolve the mystery. For years the inexperienced parents watched and waited for indications that their firstborn would begin to set things right. But the Hound of Heaven (God of explanations) was in hiding. Seasons passed, leaves fell, weeds grew, animal carcasses appeared; the curse was unrelenting. Abel joined Cain in play and arguments, laughter and tears. But the bruises and cuts brought ominous questions into the minds of the mystified Adam and Eve. What was taking so long for the Creator to reverse the curse?

Meanwhile, the individuality of the brothers was beginning to take shape, and that raised still more questions for the young parents. Why were the boys so different? They had the same parents, the same environment, the same treatment—why should they respond so differently? It was a question that would take on greater intensity as the differences in the siblings became more marked. The question plagues us still. "We've treated our children the very same. We vowed we would never play favorites. So why is that one so rebellious and his siblings so compliant?" Grappling with that question is the stock-in-trade of therapists, but the answer is elusive still. Is it a different question than God might have asked about Lucifer? How could such a perfect environment produce such rebellion? Of course, human parents make mistakes, and in spite of their best efforts, they don't treat all their children quite the same. Still, free choice that turns into rebellion has never had an easy explanation. If we could explain it, we could excuse it; but for the most part we can do neither. Free moral agents make choices—choices that hurt themselves and those who love them. When children make choices that hurt themselves and their parents, the parents often search their own past for explanations. But it is usually the wrong search. Persons who come of age can rarely plead diminished responsibility. Cain's choices were not directly the fault of his parents, though they probably berated themselves mercilessly.

The exact nature of Cain's rebellion is far from clear. It comes into focus in the setting of an offering or sacrifice. As sometimes happens in the selective history of Scripture, background explanations and rationale, which may have been crystal clear to the participants, are not always included for the benefit of future readers. While this first reference to animal sacrifice comes suddenly into the picture with no explanations, subsequent references to the ritual make its meaning clear. Furthermore, the Lord's question "If you do well, will you not be accepted?" implies that Cain knew more than is revealed in the scriptural account. "Cain brought to the Lord an offering of the fruit of the ground. . . . But for Cain and his offering [the Lord] had no regard. So Cain was very angry" (Gen. 4:3-5, RSV). It seems incongruous that any part of approaching God can be twisted into a part of the process of rebelling against Him. But from the very earliest of times humans have demonstrated a great rigidity and intolerance in their understanding of God and how to approach Him. Once a person hammers out a concept of God and a procedure of worship, other practices are not only rejected but are often vilified. "Can you believe what those people do in their worship service?" Cain knew how he wanted to approach God, and contrary suggestions he not only rejected but despised. The terse statement that the Lord did not regard Cain's offering but accepted Abel's forces us to conclude that either God is arbitrary and plays favorites, or else He had explained His expectations and Cain was arrogantly ignoring them. Surely the latter is the more likely. So while tolerance on our part is important, when God spells out His expectations we should not be surprised if human substitutions and innovations are not accepted.

But this emphasizes the great importance of these two offerings. In fact, that which gives rise to the whole tragic story is the difference in the offerings of the boys. Apparently, what humans present to God as offerings is very important. Cain brought the "fruit of the ground," and Abel brought "the firstlings of his flock" (verses 3, 4). Some similarity in work and sacrifice was represented by the two offerings, but there was also a great difference. On the one hand, there was a death, and on the other, merely human effort. In view of the consequences of Adam and Eve's sin ("cursed is the ground because of you" [Gen. 3:17, RSV]), Cain's fruit no doubt came from hard work and human effort. But that is precisely why it was unacceptable. The most conscientious human effort that produces the most perfect fruit imaginable is simply the wrong offering. Here, at the very start of redemptive history, the lesson should have been clear: it is not how much effort humans put into their gifts to God; rather, it is their acknowledgment that another life must be substituted for their own. It is a humbling acknowledgment—one that Cain did not want to make. Instead, he set out on a path of his own choosing that could never lead him to the destination he desired. But, of course, self-importance is the most common thicket that ensnares human travelers. It manifests itself in various ways, but it is always close at hand. For Cain it was a matter of bringing the best of his produce and telling God, "In my judgment that should be good enough." Today we may be tempted to give God our theological correctness as an offering instead of a daily confession that His life and His instruction must stand in the place of my life and my opinions.

It is most instructive that while God did not "regard" Cain's offering, no punitive action followed. The burden was all on Cain to come to terms with God and His requirements. But it is always humbling to say, "I was wrong," and the human ego has apparently been pushy from the very beginning. Though Cain is rapidly plunging into the thicket of selfishness, the Hound of Heaven [Lord] makes a valiant attempt to call him back from disaster. It is not too late; he can still be accepted. "If you do well, will you not be accepted? And if you do not do well, sin is crouching at the door; . . . but you must master it" (Gen. 4:7, RSV). How insistent and patient is that heavenly voice. From the beginning of time He has made it clear that He will not give up on a single human, but will follow all of them into any wilderness if there is the slightest redemptive possibility.

Instead of submitting to correction, Cain let his ego get in the way, and his anger flared—against God, no doubt. But what can you do with your anger toward God? Take it out on humans, of course. And the human that seemed to stand in the place of God, rebuking Cain by his actions, was Abel. So Cain did the logical though tragically passionate thing. With cold premeditation he invited his brother out to a field, where in a rage he attacked him. Since no one had seen or experienced human death, Cain may not have planned to kill Abel, but that hardly makes him guiltless. While the act may have been impulsive, it suggests that there had been a history of resentment that now flamed into hatred and finally murder. But if he was attempting to quiet the accusing voice, he was unsuccessful. To his surprise, the voice was unaffected. And while it carried an ominous tone, its message was not yet a final punishment. Given the enormity of his crime, is it possible that the final dialogue still contained a redemptive message? We cannot tell. One thing is certain: Cain's attitude is now hard and unrepentant. He will admit no guilt. To the Lord's question "Where is Abel?" Cain's flip response included a lie ("I don't know"), and an implication that the Lord should know better than to ask such an absurd question ("You should know that I am not my brother's guardian").

The discovery of the crime by Adam and Eve is beyond imagining. While the earlier promise, that Eve's seed would crush the serpent's head, remained maddeningly mysterious, the first couple must have cherished some vague hope that one of their sons would somehow help reverse the results of their disobedience. But now the compliant one lies still, his blood oozing into the soil, while Cain slinks off into hiding. Now what? Belatedly they now remember some of those other words the Lord had used, how there would be enmity between their seed and the serpent's seed. Little had they suspected that that enmity would actually be demonstrated in their own children. It must have been another tragic dawning of awareness as they began to suspect that their terrible mistake was not going to be fixed any time soon. The depth of their grief and the flow of their tears are inexplicably passed over by the Bible writer. Perhaps part of the reason is that no words would do justice to such emotion.

The remainder of Cain's life is largely mystery. His move "from the presence of the Lord" (verse 16) to the land of Nod (which meant "wandering") tells us little. If we view these biblical stories as attempting to set out a thorough, historical narrative of the time, we will be repeatedly frustrated and disappointed, for the gaps are frequent and intriguing. It is an approach that must find clear answers to such questions as "Where did Cain find a woman to marry who was not a relative?" "If the biblical account of the first family is true, didn't Cain have to marry his sister?" However, such a question goes beyond the purpose of the biblical narrative. The Bible stories were not meant to comprise a complete documentary. They are rather like a series of film clips. A scene pops up before us: action, sometimes brief, sometimes detailed and thorough; then, often, some sort of application. Frequently the meaning, the application, and the moral are left for us to figure out. Details that do not in some way clarify or advance the lesson of the story, no matter how much curiosity they may raise, are left frequently to our fertile imaginations. "To the religious purpose of the narrative all other things are made tributary" (*International Standard Bible Encyclopedia* [Chicago: Howard-Severance Co., 1915], Vol. I, p. 539). Did Cain marry his sister? The answer has no bearing on the story, so the question is not raised, let alone answered. What Scripture doesn't mention is usually pointless to debate.

At times, however, the narrative includes seemingly innocuous little details that make quiet curiosity difficult. For example, this story leaves raising the question of Cain's wife entirely with the reader. But it tosses into the narrative an intriguing reference to a mark the Lord puts on Cain so no one who might recognize him would kill him. What mark? Why tell us this? And why is his life spared when the rule of capital punishment (Gen. 9:6) seems to fit his case precisely?

We simply must be content with what is revealed and not let the unrevealed distract us from the larger message. The nature of the mark is left silent, but its purpose is to protect him from the very fate he had inflicted on his brother. It was a heavy sentence, from which comes the ominous phrase "He is a marked man." Why didn't he have to pay with his life, even though that was the Old Testament law? Some possible answers come to mind. The law of a life for a life was not spelled out until after the Flood story. Furthermore, it stated that "by man shall his [the murderer's] blood be shed" (verse 6, RSV). At the time of Cain's crime, who would carry out the sentence of death? In addition to all he had suffered, could God ask Adam to take the life of his only remaining son? It is the first of many examples of God's priority list, in which laws are made to serve the good of people, not the other way around. God's compassion for Adam and the continuing lessons to be learned from a live Cain apparently transcended the normal process of justice, which under different circumstances might have mandated Cain's death.

The sad story ends with Cain walking off into the distance to a land simply called Nod. He is promised a hard life. To this point his work had been to till the soil, but now, for him, the ground is doubly cursed since he has caused it to receive his brother's blood. "When you till the ground, it shall no longer yield to you its strength" (Gen. 4:12, RSV). And so he will be a wanderer, a homeless person, but one whom everyone will recognize. An endless humiliation. There are fates worse than death. And so Cain lived out his days, a constant reminder that an offering of human works, no matter how good or how perfect, is the wrong offering. A constant reminder that only a lamb's spilled blood can solve the sin problem. A constant reminder that the God of heaven and earth values free choice above coercion, even when He knows that the consequences may be disastrous. A constant reminder that even as we secretly plan our various rebellions, God knows and by His Spirit reasons with us and cautions us and woos us toward the right. A constant reminder that even as the unrepentant walk away, God's eyes track them and His loving heart follows them even into their land of wandering. A constant reminder that even when our final answer is no, He will never stop caring for us. In the words of Peter: "[Cast] all your care upon him; for he careth for you" (1 Peter 5:7). "I will never leave thee, nor forsake thee" (Heb. 13:5).

CHAPTER 3

ABRAHAM AND SARAH:
Called to Wander

EVEN AFTER PERFECTLY CLEAR INSTRUCTIONS, we sometimes make wrong turns and get lost. Sometimes an honest mistake puts us on the wrong street. Sometimes our dilemma results from negligence; other times it's the result of stubbornness or poor choices or egos that won't stop to ask directions. Whatever the cause, when we get badly lost someone or some map has to come to our aid and show us the way back. Of course, this scenario assumes that we start well and later go wrong. Like Adam and Eve. They began very well. They were certainly in the right place to begin with; but then, as a result of terrible choices and pride, they wandered away and got very lost. Not long after sin became well entrenched on our planet, there were people who were apparently in the wrong place to begin with and didn't know it. At least their locality was wrong if they were to fit in and cooperate with the purposes of God. For them the Hound of Heaven had an unusual task. Instead of tracking them down in some self-chosen thicket of disobedience, He had to lead them out of a far country of blissful ignorance and into a new land, appropriate for His purposes.

In far-off Ur, that dusty settlement in what is today southern Iraq, a man by the name of Abram heard the mysterious call to start wandering north. Apparently he and his clan were in the wrong place for God's purposes, but they were blissfully ignorant about it. But as the heavenly voice gained clarity, Abram gathered up his family, and with the rest of his entourage made it as far as Haran, north of Palestine.

There they lived for some years in a state of mystified ignorance, knowing this was not the final destination, but also wondering what the final destination was. With the death of his father, Terah, Abram promptly heard the call to wander south to Canaan.

The call to wander some more must have seemed an unusual call for Abram and his family. In our time that call seems especially strange, given that Abram was 75 years of age. If you were picking someone for a long and difficult travel adventure, you would probably pick someone young and vigorous, and age 75 just doesn't seem that young and vigorous. In fact, a man that age strikes us as more of an elder statesman than a long-distance explorer. At that age, if someone is in unusually good physical condition, we start tacking on the qualifier "for a person of his/her age." But *elderly* means different things at different times. Terah, Abram's father, lived to be 200 and was 70 when he had three sons. Given such vigor, Abram at 75 could probably undertake a difficult trip. And it was difficult. "Go from your country and your kindred and your father's house to the land that I will show you" (Gen. 12:1, RSV). This is not just a trip; it is a major uprooting. I have come to dread major moves. The excitement of new scenery and a new position is quickly replaced by the drudgery of boxes, bare cupboards, and unlivable rooms. "That room is ready for the movers, so we'll just have to stay out of it for a few days." Then there is the frustration of missing familiar objects for months, or even years, because they got crammed quickly into some of those unlabeled boxes just as the moving van was pulling in. Big moves are for the young and energetic. Presumably the 75-year-old Abram was still energetic, if not so young.

In addition to all the other difficulties, it was a move into the dark. I cannot quite identify with Abram's call to wander off toward an unknown land. Our family has moved many times, but we have yet to pack up our things for a completely unknown destination. True, Abram probably figured he was headed for Canaan; still, the move that began in Ur, and that would eventually lead to what is modern Palestine, was a lot like flying blind. Hebrews 11:8 adds the terse comment, "not knowing where he was to go" (RSV).

But the destination was only part of the puzzle, and a small part at that. There was also the mysterious promise that God would bless him abundantly and make him into a "great nation" (Gen. 12:2). It was mysterious because of a brief comment that just preceded the narrative about the long trip. "Now Sarai was barren; she had no child" (Gen. 11:30, NRSV). To make a nation you have to have people; and people all start out as babies; and babies come from fertile wives, not barren ones. In Old Testament times, if children did not come readily into a family, the fault was virtually always attributed to the wife's inability to conceive. In that time and place the possibility of male infertility was hard for them even to imagine. This is not to suggest that Abram's lack of an heir was his doing. It only points up the pressure that continued to build on Sarai. Even without the promise, a great deal of weight was on her shoulders to produce a male heir. But now comes this promise. A great nation? Something would have to change.

We need to take another look or two at this twosome. Typical of this time, Sarai gets very little press, even though her role will be crucial to the success of the promise. In six different settings from Genesis 12 to 22 the promise of a son and many descendants is repeated to Abram, but not once to Sarai. When she finally did hear about her role, it was because she eavesdropped (Gen. 18:10, 11). Abram, on the other hand, gets all the press. Furthermore, thanks in large part to Paul and James, we have developed a beautiful but rather one-dimensional view of Abram. Since he is referred to as the "father of all them that believe" (Rom. 4:11), we rarely see his character completely filled in. While he passed several great tests of faith, he also failed a few. Not that this fact should diminish the man or his life of faith. Instead, it should remind us that a person of faith is, at the same time, a developing believer, a believer with flaws, a believer from among the human race, a believer who needed the Hound of Heaven as much as the rest of us.

The humanity of this man of faith is forcibly brought home in a few short verses. In Genesis 12:4 he responds to God's call with faith and obedience and leaves Haran for some unknown homestead in Canaan. He finds a suitable spot, pitches his tent, builds an altar to the Lord, and prepares to settle in. But his wandering is not over. Later (verse 10) he is headed south to Egypt to escape famine. At this point the Hound of Heaven is like a leader dog leading its blind charges through one mystery after another. Perhaps it shouldn't surprise us that Abram occasionally loses patience, lets go of his leader dog, and strikes out on his own. In the process he tables his trust in God and sets the stage for an ignominious humiliation. "Since you are so beautiful," he tells Sarai, "let's lead the Egyptians to think you are not my wife, so it will go well with *me,* that *my* life may be spared" (see verses 11-13). So much for the father of the faithful. His plan sounds like straightforward self-serving. There is no indication that Abram consults Sarai about her wishes or willingness to attempt such deception. If the ruse were to be uncovered, was her life or safety not at risk? Whatever his motive, his lack of trust, instead of helping to advance God's plan, puts the entire plan in jeopardy. As Trevor Dennis put it: "If there is a villain of this piece, . . . it is not the pharaoh, but Abram" (*Sarah Laughed* [Nashville: Abingdon Press, 1994], p. 38).

The surprising upshot of the near disaster is that Abram gets rich. Pharaoh did indeed deal well with Abram because of Sarai, and gave him all kinds of herd animals and even servants (verse 16). It appears Pharaoh felt that the honorable thing was to pay Sarai's "brother" a kind of dowry. It must have taken days for the transaction to be complete. Should Abram have accepted the money, and continued the deception? Of course not. But after starting down the road of deceit, it is always difficult to know when to backpedal. Throughout the process Sarai is treated like a pawn who has no choice but to be "taken into Pharaoh's house" (verse 15). How long did Abram allow the intolerable situation to exist? Did he wait a day, two days, three days? We know enough time passed for God to afflict Pharaoh's house with great plagues (verse 17). Did they come in one night, or is this a clue that it took Abram a while to figure out how to get out of the mess he had made?

It is a bit shocking to consider that the ethics of the heathen pharaoh seem to outstrip those of faithful Abram. Not that we approve of Pharaoh's harem. That idea grates on our understanding of Christian marriage ethics. But in a time when God apparently winked at the foolishness of Hebrew concubines, we probably should not get too bellicose at heathen harems. But putting that to one side, this pharaoh's sense of right and wrong shames the ethics of "faithful" Abram. Pharaoh has paid a large sum in the legal process of acquiring Abram's "sister." He thinks it is all open and aboveboard, especially since Abram has accepted the gifts. But it has all happened because of an intentional deception perpetrated by a man who isn't sure God can provide for his safety. In "faithful" Abram, as in all believers, trust and doubt are occasional bedfellows.

"Why did you say, 'She is my sister,' so that I took her for my wife?" (verse 19, NRSV). Were he a less scrupulous man, Pharaoh surely would not have paid a high price for her to begin with, and he certainly would not be having this reproving dialogue with the deceptive stranger from the north. Given the pharaoh's familiarity with power politics, it is not a small surprise that he lets sneaky Abram off so easy. It would seem more in character for him to confront Abram with his deception, and then promptly execute him. Instead, after an extremely short tongue-lashing, he curtly responds, "Here is your wife, take her, and be gone" (verse 19, NRSV). Pretty mild stuff. After all, Abram has treated Sarai as a mere object through whom he has been able to manipulate Pharaoh. Then, too, he has treated Pharaoh with disdain, allowing him to embarrass himself and be afflicted with the plagues of God. Furthermore, he has certainly put God's whole plan in jeopardy, because if his ruse were discovered, he must have realized that Pharaoh would probably kill him, boot the rest of his entourage out of Egypt, and thereby send God's plan for a great nation back to the drawing board. In spite of Abram's duplicity, however, God intervenes, and the entire group is allowed to leave Egypt in much better shape than when they entered. A famine had driven them to this land, hungry and empty-handed. Because of Abram's deception, their stay was cut very short; yet when they left, "Abram was very rich in cattle, in silver, and in gold" (Gen. 13:2, RSV). And all of that thanks to a dutiful, patient wife, a pharaoh with a sense of morals, and, of course, that Hunting Hound who never lets us out of His sight.

The Hound and His interventions take unusual forms. In this case He brought about great plagues (Gen. 12:17). But His tactics run the gamut from taming lions to guiding sling stones to stopping flowing rivers. The only constant is that the approach He takes is always appropriate for the occasion. In this story, His impact on the pharaoh was truly amazing—he took the moral high ground right away. He might not have. Some years later another pharaoh was afflicted with "great plagues," and his response was to harden his heart until his whole country was in ruins. When this pharaoh felt the hot breath of heaven, his sense of right and wrong surfaced immediately. One thing is clear: it is difficult to pull Abram through this experience and make him look good. He comes across looking chauvinistic, self-serving, and short on faith. Sarai, in contrast, comes through looking very much the helpless pawn—told just what to say, dutifully obeying, taken into Pharaoh's house, then shuttled back to her husband and removed from the country by her husband and his relatives. Through it all, she is asked nothing and says nothing. It's as if she has done nothing of her own volition, only had things done to her.

The following chapters in Abram's life show him hustling about, resolving conflicts between his servants and those of Lot. He walks all over the countryside surveying things (Gen. 13:17), goes to war to get Lot out of serious trouble (Gen. 14:15), and then pays tithe of all the booty to a mysterious figure called Melchizedek (verse 18). Interspersed through all the frenetic activity are numerous reassurances that the covenant between God and Abram is in place and "your reward shall be very great" (Gen. 15:1, RSV). Of course, Abram doesn't understand what this means, and Sarai knows even less. God sees it all, but they must keep walking in the dark.

Genesis 16 reintroduces Sarai, but what an introduction! Who likes to be introduced by a negative? "I'd like you to meet my friend, Sarai, who can't have a baby." "Now Sarai, Abram's wife, bore him no children" (verse 1, RSV). Ten years have gone by since they settled in Canaan (verse 3), and for Sarai the boundary markers for those 10 years are two references to her barrenness. It must have been a shattering embarrassment. Now at last, after all that time has gone by, she is brought back into focus by means of a reminder that she can't bear a child. Then for the very first time in this 10-year period she is finally given a voice. Is it any wonder that her first recorded words focus on the problem that has become her preoccupation and her shame? How much longer than 10 years they have been married is not clear, but given the cultural expectations of the time, that is a very long time to wait for the first child. Through all that time there is no indication that Sarai was aware of all the promises to Abram of a large family. In fact, her surprise, when she overhears the word in Genesis 18, hints that up to that point she has been in the dark regarding any future family. In any case, 10 years of barrenness are more than enough, and she is ready to do almost anything for a child.

Her longing for children had nothing to do with helping work out God's plan, because she didn't know there was a plan. Her scheme centers entirely on her own sense of reproach for not having borne a son to Abram. She suggests a surrogate arrangement whereby her maid, Hagar, will step into the void and "I shall obtain children by her" (Gen. 16:2, RSV). At this point Sarai appears as a thoroughly modern woman. The financial arrangement and the legal implications were different than today's, but the concept of surrogacy is certainly up-to-date. Children born of a slave were considered the property of the owner of the slave woman, so Sarai's idea seemed to be a natural and simple solution to her dilemma.

When Sarai comes up with a scheme to help resolve her embarrassment, Abram suddenly comes across as the compliant one. After 10-plus years we know only two things about Sarai: she is the wife of Abram, and she can't have children. Beyond that, all is speculation. But suddenly she has a voice and a plan and the full support of her husband. Does he cooperate because he feels it is a good idea or simply because it is an idea, something he is fresh out of? Since he is the man of faith, shouldn't he say something like "No, Sarai, we must wait in faith while God works out His plan for us"? Does he honestly believe that Sarai's plan is God's method of working out the covenant promise? In any case, as is common with surrogate mothering, Sarai's version goes quickly awry, and Abram must share in the blame. He must have known the power that childbirth conferred on women in his day. Accordingly, the outcome of this incident was quite predictable. Hagar easily conceived, but whatever arrangement she had originally agreed to was quickly scotched when she held her baby. Instead of blessing Sarai with her son, "she looked with contempt on her mistress" (verse 4, RSV).

Will nothing ever go right for Sarai? Is she destined to take her barrenness, her humiliation, all the way to the grave? Those who knew her during most of her adult life would remember her for one thing: she could not conceive. How significant and instructive it is that God chose the most unlikely wife in Israel, a sterile woman, to be the most remembered mother in Israel. It seems that God enjoys tweaking the noses of those who are "slow of heart to believe" (Luke 24:25). He begins a nation of millions with a barren woman. He picks a slow-talking, ineloquent shepherd (Ex. 4:10) to confront a powerful ruler and free the slaves. A young boy defeats the giant Goliath. A virgin girl becomes the mother of the Messiah. How many examples do we need to be forever convinced of His interest in the human scene and of His ability to turn hopelessness into promise? How many times must the Hound of Heaven come to our rescue before we will relax in the knowledge of His persistence?

In her bitter disappointment at Hagar's contempt Sarai turns to Abram for help, but he is no help. Whereas before he has done all the talking and acting, now when Sarai comes up with an ill-conceived plan, Abram does nothing to keep her from falling on her face. As a result, her bitterness finally flares: "May the wrong done to me be on you! I gave my maid to your embrace, and when she saw that she had conceived, she looked on me with contempt. May the Lord judge between you and me!" (Gen. 16:15, RSV). The quiet Sarai has at last found her voice. What a voice! The years of humiliation and frustration finally boil to the surface, and she lifts up Abram's complicity for all to see. Now he is the one with little to say. Up to now he has always been the spokesman with a plan or a scheme. Suddenly he has lost his voice. All he can do is stammer out, "Your maid is in your power; do to her as you please" (verse 6, RSV). Sarai's jealousy, frustration, and smoldering resentment result in a cruel plan to banish the child she can never claim as hers. Abram's failure to intervene indicts him. In contrast, God's lifesaving intervention makes clear that Sarai's plan was not God's.

Following the sad incident of Hagar and Ishmael, the Lord again appears to Abram to renew the covenant promise about a great nation and, in the process, lengthens Abram's name to Abraham. In the same chapter Sarai's name is changed to Sarah. Some scholars maintain that the name Sarai is simply an older equivalent to Sarah. A more likely explanation is that Sarai meant "mockery," while Sarah means "princess." If so, there is a clue here that Sarah is about to come into her own. Perhaps her role is about to become more clear and take on the noble aspects that the Lord has known about all along.

Still, her belated rise to prominence has a very inauspicious beginning. Once again it is Abraham who is at the center of activity. This time the Lord appears to him in a disguise with tragic news about Sodom and Gomorrah's abbreviated future. When mysterious visitors suddenly appear at his tent door, Abraham is portrayed hustling about, trying too hard to be an engaging host (Gen. 18:2-9). He quickly orders Sarah to make cakes for the guests and has a servant dress an entire calf for the occasion, enough food for a very large meal for many people. True to Eastern custom, Sarah stays out of sight, so it must have come as a surprise to Abraham when his visitor asks, "Where is Sarah your wife?" (verse 9, RSV). Abraham responds, "In the tent," but makes no move to call her out and introduce her to them. So the Lord proceeds to talk about her as if she were not there, knowing she would hear what He said. "Sarah your wife shall have a son" (verse 10, RSV). To this menopausal woman the prospect of pregnancy had now changed from pathetic longing to a source of humor. The years of disappointment had taken their toll on her trust in God. Scripture gives no indication that she was privy to the earlier promises of family that God had repeatedly given to Abraham. This may have been the very first time she has heard the incredible promise of many descendants. In any case, it has come so late in her life that she can respond only with a cynical chuckle and perhaps something under her breath equivalent to "Yeah, right!" Still, when the heavenly visitor correctly interprets it as a laugh of disbelief, Sarah quickly denies the charge. Surprisingly, the angel chooses not to make an issue of her doubt. Years later, when the elderly Zacharias showed the same skepticism over the possible birth of his son, he was struck speechless for several months. Maybe Sarah's skepticism was better justified.

With God's promise now clear to both Abraham and Sarah, the aged couple has time simply to await the fulfillment. But when they travel south to Gerar, the behavior of Abraham is hard to believe and impossible to justify. It seems he has learned nothing from his previous duplicity with the pharaoh. His rationale, as before, is a strange mixture of self-serving, faulty assumptions, and lack of faith. Abraham assumes there is "no fear of God . . . in this place" (Gen. 20:11, RSV), so of course they will seize his 99-year-old wife because she is so physically beautiful and kill him in the process. So once again he convinces Sarah to play his sister and is again humbled, this time by Abimelech, king of Gerar. As it turns out, Abimelech was a man who was not so out of touch with God as Abraham had suspected. At least he had a rather clear bit of dialogue with God that was hardly open to debate or uncertainty.

"You're a dead man, Abimelech, for having taken a married man's wife."

"But Lord, how was I to know? They both lied to me."

"I knew it was an honest mistake—that's why you haven't yet slept with her. I knew you would do the right thing if you learned the truth."

Pretty good communication for an "unbelieving" king. He hears and believes God's warning about taking Sarah for a wife, and out of his superstitious fear he not only returns Sarah, but pays Abraham with gifts of money and real estate. The lesson to be learned is not that God keeps rewarding wrongdoing, but that He is always close at hand and consistently treats us better than we deserve. Indeed, when we least expect Him, the Hound of Heaven gives quiet hints that He is never far away. Paul helped us to look upon Abraham as the father of all true believers (Rom. 4:3, 16), but these incidents of failure also hold him up before us as an appropriate symbol of the meaning of grace and forgiveness.

God had one more test for Abraham. Remember, he hadn't been all that successful with some of his former tests, and this one would make all the others pale by comparison. The biblical account is simple and succinct—a mere 14 verses. The brevity masks the intensity and difficulty of the test. It defies belief. Several times Abraham had put the whole covenant at risk by his shortsightedness and unbelief. Now it appeared that God was doing the same thing by direct command. "Take your son, your only son Isaac, whom you love, and . . . offer him . . . as a burnt offering" (Gen. 22:2, RSV). Apparently the voice was familiar; there is no indication that Abraham argued with it or challenged its authority. But the message it brought was impossible. In fact, the words are arranged in an order that is designed to heighten the emotional attachment and make compliance with the command the most difficult possible. Just look at the phrases: "Take your son, your only son, Isaac [Isaac wasn't his only son], whom you love." This son meant the fulfillment of all the promises. What would his death mean? Nothing of any value. God is not so foolish as to contradict Himself, and He had repeatedly forbidden killing and human sacrifices. Now He was asking Abraham to do both. It cannot be—it is all a hoax.

It should not be too surprising that when Abraham was confronted by his greatest test of faith, to offer Isaac as a martyr, Sarah does not enter into the test in any way. Earlier her jealousy and punishing anger would have driven Hagar and Ishmael to a certain death of deprivation had not God intervened. That had happened when Sarah looked out a window and saw the half brothers just playing together. Given her fierce protectiveness, how could Abraham now convince her that God wanted Isaac to be the first divinely approved human sacrifice? No, it is not surprising that Abraham quietly roused Isaac and two servants "early in the morning" (Gen. 22:3). He knew he needed to leave early, before Sarah had a chance to detect anything unusual about her elderly husband's behavior. He was approximately 120 years old and probably didn't feel overly confident that he would be able to start off on his troublesome journey with Sarah looking on.

When confronted with past tests of faith, Abraham had had rather spotty success. But the great thing about the Hound of Heaven is His tenacity. He stays with His prey until He is successful or until all hope is gone. Abraham had been through a lot, but nothing could have prepared him for this last trial by fire. He had three days to agonize over its meaning, and all he drew was a blank. We can often bear up under intense pressure and make great sacrifices when it is all for a noble cause. To suffer so that someone else might not have to often seems worth the price. But to suffer some great loss for no obvious reason is unusually difficult, and Abraham could find no apparent purpose to be served by his sacrifice of Isaac. Since he could find no purpose in it, he could share nothing significant about the trip with Isaac. That must have been the hardest part of Abraham's three-day trip—trying to make small talk while keeping the real plan and destination secret. It is hardly surprising that Abraham "had no heart for words" (*Patriarchs and Prophets,* p. 151). His inner turmoil was unremitting. But then it got bumped up several degrees when Isaac asked that gut-wrenching question, "Father, we have the wood and the fire, but where is the lamb for a sacrifice?" (see Gen. 22:7).

"God will provide himself the lamb for a burnt offering, my son" (verse 8, RSV). If Abraham actually heard his own words, they must have meant nothing to him at the time. Or perhaps they were like the idle words parents often say when their kids bring up some issue that is embarrassing or ill-timed. For Abraham it was clearly a delaying tactic—hardly a prophetic utterance. But I think God likes to sprinkle His revelations with double entendres that have both local and cosmic import. Of course, for those like Abraham, who lived the events and even mouthed the words, the larger import rarely registered. But for later generations of readers, the prophetic aspect fairly leaps from the page, saying,

"This story is more than a historical account. There is a divine mind directing these events and the telling of these events. God will provide Himself the lamb." Mark it well: like Abraham, you are never out of the sight of the Hound of Heaven.

Then came the crest of Mount Moriah. No more delay. The tearful explanation that didn't really explain. Abraham moving forward blindly, in spite of the bewildering contradiction—"Human sacrifices are an abomination. . . . Take now thy son and offer him." But Abraham was familiar with the voice: he had heard it often before. His frequent communication had made that voice familiar. Consequently, there was no mistaking what he had to do. He had finally learned to trust that voice implicitly. While he didn't understand the how or when or why of resurrection, he believed that it could happen. "By faith Abraham, when he was tested, offered up Isaac. . . . He considered that God was able to raise men even from the dead; hence, figuratively speaking, he did receive him back" (Heb. 11:17-19, RSV). So although the angel stopped the action before there was any bloodshed, in Abraham's intent he plunged the knife into his son's chest. His trust in that familiar voice was now complete, and the snared ram in the nearby thicket rewarded that trust.

God's response to Abraham is more than a little troubling at first thought. "Now I know that you fear God, seeing you have not withheld your son" (Gen. 22:12, RSV). Is that what this prolonged nightmare was all about—to convince God of something He wasn't sure of? Really? God, who sees all and knows all, put this old man through this agonizing test to see if this man He has known for 120 years will obey? You mean God still wasn't sure what Abraham would do? Since God is all-knowing, should He have said, "Of course, I knew all along that you would pass the test"? To which Abraham might have replied, "Then why was it so important to put me through it?" To which God might answer, "Because you and a lot of other people would be able to see, more clearly than ever before, the contours of trusting, saving faith. As Ellen White puts it: "The sacrifice required of Abraham was not alone for his own good, nor solely for the benefit of succeeding generations; but it was also for the instruction of the sinless intelligences of heaven and of other worlds" (*Patriarchs and Prophets,* p. 154). So perhaps God was saying, "Now I have seen demonstrated what I have known all along, that your faith would eventually come to this level of trust. But also, now you know by experience, and millions of onlookers and readers can know the contours of mature faith."

Both Abraham and Sarah had lived their long lives learning the meaning of trusting faith in God. It had been a spotty process; but, at long last, the message had gotten through, the lesson learned. Perhaps that explains why Abraham felt compelled to name the spot Jehovah-jireh: "the Lord will provide." On that remote hill Abraham confesses the truth that made him worthy to be called the "father of all them that believe," no matter the circumstances: "the Lord will provide." Or to put it another way, there is no spot on earth or situation in life in which God can't track us down and provide a "ram in the thicket."

Of course, the selection of that mountain, that event, and that divine intervention had about it an appropriateness that far surpassed anything that Abraham could have imagined. How could he have ever conjured up the scene that would take place on that very hill hundreds of years later? Never could he have imagined that in a great temple, built on that very spot, a whole system of sacrifices would be celebrated and then come to fruition with the death of the only Lamb that ever really mattered, the Lamb of God. Jehovah-jirah, "the Lord will provide." Will He ever!

CHAPTER 4

JACOB AND ESAU:
The Troubled Twins

FOR YEARS SHE FEARED she would never have a child. No doubt Rebekah's fears were magnified by the oft-repeated story of her mother-in-law. Sarah's barrenness had become a legend. No one could explain the miraculous, postmenopausal birth of Isaac. Now it appears the cycle is being repeated as Rebekah, like her mother-in-law, is considered barren (Gen. 25:21). It almost seems as if the Lord enjoys setting up impossible situations so He can show us how easily He deals with them. So when the time was right, the God who has always known about fertility drugs got involved; and the result was the very first recorded multiple births. When God cures barrenness, He does it with flair. He does lots of things with flair.

But while God made the conception easy, the pregnancy was something else. In fact, it became what we would call a crisis pregnancy. It got so bad that Rebekah came to despair of life itself. "If it is thus, why do I live?" (verse 22, RSV). If it had been today's scene, would the subject of abortion have come up? Did the thought ever cross Rebekah's mind? We can never know. What she didn't know, of course, was that she was about to bear the very first twin boys. What she did know was that whatever was in utero was about to do her in. But then the Lord explained to her that her twins would each found a nation of people (verse 23). In time this fact would become important to her, but few mothers who suffer difficulties in late pregnancy spend time waxing philosophical about the distant future and their child's role in it. Still, it must have been somewhat reassuring for Rebekah to hear that her prenatal pains would result in babies with auspicious destinies.

Then came the births and more trouble. Indications had already hinted that nothing about the boys was going to be routine. The naming seemed to be the easiest part. The first one was named for his looks (Esau, "red one"), while the second one was named for his actions (Jacob, "heel grabber"). As the boys' personalities developed, each parent bonded with just one: Isaac, with Esau; and Rebekah, with Jacob. Unfortunately, that parental favoritism contributed to a sibling split that would eventually bring unremitting grief to the entire family.

Of course, sibling rivalry didn't start with Jacob and Esau. Cain and Abel had already demonstrated that phenomenon. These twins, however, had an additional complication—a parental tug-of-war. Was their development shaped by that factor? Probably. Still, to understand fully just what caused the twins to take such divergent paths is not an easy assignment. In this story, as in so many others, the Bible writers seem little interested in giving us much information about childhood influences, so we don't get to know them as boys. Apparently neither boy was murderous like Cain, but their values were clearly negotiable. In addition, Esau was brash and impulsive; Jacob was devious and cunning. The first recorded incident took place when they were already young men. Esau, returning from the field, was hungry—to the point of death (verses 30, 32); and Jacob had just cooked up a batch of "red stuff." So the trap was set, and Jacob was eager to spring it. Jacob, greedy for the birthright, capitalized on his twin's desperation; and Esau, looking with disdain on his birthright, bargained it away for a dish of soup. The deal was struck: Jacob got the birthright, and Esau got the porridge. But a wedge had been driven between the boys.

Of course, the twins were surrounded by people who set questionable examples. In fact, the family tree had a history of compromising standards. Twice Grandpa Abraham had attempted to deceive people about Sarah's relationship to him. Then Isaac bore out the old maxim "like father like son"—for he told the same lie to the same Philistine king (Gen. 26:7). Later mother Rebekah would show that she was not above chicanery and deception when she convinced Jacob to trick his nearly blind father into giving him, instead of Esau, the cherished blessing. Perhaps it was Jacob's act of deception that gave birth to the phrase "pulling the wool over one's eyes," for that is quite literally what Jacob did to convince his father that he was Esau. Rebekah's trickery would soon be bested by her brother Laban's various shenanigans and tawdry treatment of Jacob. Where did these Hebrews learn their ethics? Just how many times will the Hound of Heaven have to come searching the thickets to get these wayward ones back on track?

It may come as a shock to some that when we look behind the closed doors of biblical families, one near constant is the high level of pain and stress created by straying children. The present story is a prime example. "When Esau was forty years old, he took to wife Judith the daughter of Beeri the Hittite, and Basemath the daughter of Elon the Hittite; and they made life bitter for Isaac and Rebekah" (verse 34, RSV). A close look at many of the early families reveals that the hurts, heartaches, and rewards of parenting have changed little over the centuries. Biblical families agonized over youthful folly and sibling rivalry that often escalated into hatred and even murder. The close father-son relationship of Abraham and Isaac clearly seems to be the exception rather than the rule. More often there are scenes of bewildered, grieving parents wondering what they could have done wrong. The Hound of Heaven had lots of tracking to do, often with apparently marginal success. It should bring some comfort to today's parents who grope for explanations for their seeming failures, and who feel that no genuine Christian parents should ever produce a wayward child. Yet to a large degree that is really the only kind of children flawed parents can produce. Only by the grace of a very patient God can we ever expect our children to become heirs of the kingdom, and sometimes that may happen in spite of us parents, not because of us.

Rebekah hardly set a good example before her children. As mentioned, she was the mastermind behind Jacob's deception of his father. Unfortunately, her plan misfired as she tragically underestimated the bitter reaction of Esau. Perhaps she assumed that Esau would care little about the blessing. After all, when the twins struck that earlier deal and Esau chose porridge over privilege, he "despised his birthright" (Gen. 25:34). But the passage of time served as heat that inexorably caused his anger to boil up into murderous proportions. "The days of mourning for my father are approaching; then I will kill my brother Jacob" (Gen. 27:41, RSV).

As Esau's anger simmered and his plan leaked out, Rebekah had to quickly come up with plan B. It became another of her schemes to save her favorite twin. By now they are grown; Esau has married badly, and continues to bring grief to his parents. His threat to rid the earth of his brother when Isaac dies strikes terror in Rebekah's heart, so she hatches a plan to get Jacob out of the territory and into safer regions. She feels she has to convince Isaac, not so much because he would object to Jacob's leaving (after all, Esau was his favorite), but because she needed to conceal Esau's murderous intentions. She keeps some of the facts fuzzy by focusing Isaac's attention on Esau's bad marriages. If Jacob repeats his brother's bad choices and marries a local Hittite girl, it would be more than either parent can bear (Gen. 27:46). Accordingly it would be far better for him to marry a good cousin than a bad Hittite. Rebekah makes her case so well that Isaac is the one who calls Jacob and informs him that he must not marry locally, but must go to his uncle Laban's household in Paddan-aram and pick one of his cousins to marry (Gen. 28:1, 2). No doubt Jacob played his part well, probably even acting surprised, even though his mother had already told him he was going to have to leave. So he left, and his doting mother would never see him again. His return 20 years later would be too late; Rebekah would be dead. Wrong choices often result in severe consequences.

Jacob's trip north to Haran was eventful. Somewhere on the way, during the quiet of the night, a voice "beat more instant than the Feet." The Hound of Heaven was on the prowl, and the result was a thrilling affirmation that Jacob had a future—that God had not given up on him, despite his deceitfulness and opportunism of the past. "And he dreamed that there was a ladder set up on the earth, the top of it reaching to heaven; and the angels of God were ascending and descending on it. And the Lord stood beside him" (verses 12, 13, NRSV). In the midst of his lonely journey that dream brought encouragement and a new sense of hope to the bewildered Jacob as he pondered what his life had become and where it was headed.

Like Jacob, we too have nights of crises. They come to us with many different faces, and sometimes, as with Jacob, they are of our own making, though knowing that does little to lessen our despair. Thoughts of pleasure couple with weakness, and a baby is conceived out of wedlock. The future grandparents are embarrassed and critical. Fear, guilt, and finally despair all take a heavy toll. Our night is black and our wilderness barren. No one sympathizes. We are truly alone and a very long way from home or heaven. A test result comes back positive. The doctor quietly says, "I'm so sorry. I wish I could do more." Our tears well up. No one can really understand, though they all say they do. You feel totally alone. But the message of Jacob's dream makes it clear that no night is so dark and no crisis so dire that we are beyond the reach of heaven's ladder or lost to Heaven's Hound. Yet how quickly and how often we forget.

But the self-serving Jacob, who had played fast and loose with his own principles, now receives one of the most reassuring and far-reaching promises in all of Scripture. "Know that I am with you and will keep you wherever you go and will bring you back to this land; for I will not leave you until I have done what I have promised you" (verse 15, NRSV). And why was God so involved, so caring? Was it because Jacob had earned God's favor by a life of obedience? Or was it because He is a God of grace who always treats us better than we deserve? Jacob is overwhelmed. But of course that is the only appropriate response when grace hits home. There is always that unexpected, unanticipated, completely undeserved aspect to grace. "Surely the Lord is in this place; and I did not know it" (verse 16, RSV). Is grace not at the heart of such a confession? This story should make us wonder if God is ever very far removed from us. Or to put it another way: when our leaden prayers seem to sink into nothingness instead of rise to God, it must be our own distractions and self-absorption that isolate us—not some physical distance from God. In the words of the song: "If God's not there, guess who went away?"

In his flushed, almost breathless response Jacob bursts out with a statement of worship. "How awesome is this place! This is none other than the house of God, and this is the gate of heaven" (verse 17, RSV). What a statement about an out-of-the-way corner of some rocky field in mid-Palestine. Apparently the gate of heaven is not limited to some distant spot in space like the constellation Orion. The gate of heaven is our back porch, or a quiet meadow, or some out-of-the-way place that we least expect.

Jacob's act of worship included making an altar out of his pillow/rock. As he did so, he proceeded to translate his grateful surprise into the form of a vow. But the vow reflects an immature faith that is conditioned on

God's continuing to be good to him. A vow that begins with an "if" clause is not yet an unconditional, trusting faith. "If God will be with me, and will keep me . . . , and will give me bread to eat and clothing to wear, . . . then the Lord shall be my God, and . . . I will surely give one tenth to you" (verses 20, 21, NRSV). Jacob had some maturing to do.

How often we make the same kind of offer to God. "Lord, if You will just . . . , then I will . . . " "For just one answered prayer, Lord, I will then believe You care." "If You will heal my daughter's cancer . . ." Faith that is based on a condition is not yet faith at all.

Jacob's arrival at Uncle Laban's household turned out to be all that he had hoped it would be—and more. I have never been particularly inclined to kiss any of my cousins, but Jacob found it rather easy not only to help Cousin Rachel with her sheep, but kiss her as well. Of course, it helped that she was "beautiful and lovely" (Gen. 29:17, RSV). And apparently it was more than superficial beauty. There is a patina that wears off quickly, but Rachel's beauty was inside as well as outside. And Jacob soon found himself making incredible promises so that he could have her hand in marriage. Seven years he would be willing to work for her. Seven years! Laban agrees—why would he not?—and that wonderfully romantic passage follows: "And they seemed to him but a few days because of the love he had for her" (Gen. 29:20, RSV). Love can cover blemishes and diminish unpleasantness and even speed up the passage of time.

What follows is the rather detailed account of the various acts of treachery and deceit between uncle and nephew, who also becomes the son-in-law. First Uncle Laban deceives his son-in-law-to-be about the most prized gift in life: his beautiful bride. Then Jacob frets over how he can develop some independence and provide for his growing family. Since the means of exchange was flocks, not money, he hammered out a deal with his father-in-law. As the flocks increased, Jacob could keep all the lambs and goats that were born imperfectly colored—the spotted and black ones—and Laban would keep all the perfect white ones. Fair enough. Except that after this arrangement was made, Laban went through the flock and took out for himself all the animals that would build up Jacob's agreed-upon spotted ones (Gen. 30:35). Clearly Laban was not the kind of man people would choose to do business with. But of course Jacob was caught, and Laban attempted to keep Jacob indebted to him for life. He changed his wages 10 times (Gen. 31:41), and the context indicates that those were not raises.

At the same time, Jacob was not the kind to cower and remain content in his position as the exploited victim. He could scheme with the best of them. In fact, the scheme he devised was only a slight cut above the level of his uncle's ethics. While Laban had overtly removed the animals that would most contribute to Jacob's success, Jacob was more subtle. He devised a scheme that would rapidly increase his animals, at the expense of Laban, by putting various colored stakes in the ground around the watering troughs where the animals bred. Seeing spots while they bred would produce lambs and young goats that were spotted and variegated, rather than all white (Gen. 30:37-43). With our knowledge of genetics, the whole idea seems bizarre and unreal; but for reasons that elude us, it seemed to work. Jacob's spotted animals began a rapid increase, while Laban's did not. Jacob did nothing illegal, just devious. What a scene. One devious schemer attempting to outwit another; rogue competing with rogue.

What a context for the formation of the most famous family ever to walk the earth—a family whose descendants are identifiable still. For it was during these years that Jacob, later known as Israel, was fathering his 10 sons by four women: his two wives and their two maids. These were the difficult years for Jacob. But the middle years are difficult for many families. Raising our children, paying the bills, getting established, and finding our place in the world are basic and difficult enough, but we are also made to feel that being a success includes contributing something positive to society. The resulting pressure often leaves little time for other important activities such as courting your spouse, playing with the kids, and spending time with God. The daily routine can become a daily grind that results in weariness and a gradually increasing distance between us and God. A grinding cynicism develops.

Such was the case with Jacob. With a family grown large, he still slaved away, literally, at his work for his father-in-law, with little opportunity to develop his own independence. Later, as he is summing up this time, he tells Laban, "By day the heat consumed me, and the cold by night, and my sleep fled from my eyes. These twenty years I have been in your house; I served you fourteen years for your two daughters, and six years for your flock, and you have changed my wages ten times. If the God of my father, the God of Abraham . . . , had not been on my side, surely now you would have sent me away empty-handed" (Gen. 31:40-42, RSV). Somehow he had to escape the clutches of his self-serving uncle—but where could he go? His home territory beckoned, but his murderous brother still lived there. For his own self-esteem he simply had to leave Haran, but at what price Palestine? His options were maddeningly simple: an empty shell of a life in Haran, or death at the hands of his brother.

But as we have seen, and as Jacob should have remembered, it is into such overwhelming dilemmas that the Hound of Heaven delights to enter. How frequently God allows the night to first become totally dark, so as to accent the brightness of His light. So in the darkness of his circumstances, when his problems seemed completely insurmountable, the Lord sent His angel, who simply told Jacob, "Now arise, go forth from this land, and return to the land of your birth" (verse 13, RSV). Only after that divine directive could Jacob summon the courage to pack up his considerable family and leave. But he had to do it with subterfuge. Laban was so controlling that Jacob waited until Laban was away shearing his sheep, and then "Jacob outwitted Laban . . . , in that he did not tell him that he intended to flee" (verse 20, RSV). When Laban got the word three days later, he lost no time catching up with Jacob to haul him back, except that the Lord again intervened and warned Laban to let Jacob completely alone in his decision. The result was an amicable parting with a stone pillar to mark the spot and be a constant reminder that it was the Lord who had brought peace between them: "The Lord watch between you and me, when we are absent one from the other" (verse 49, RSV).

But one more crisis loomed before Jacob and his family could settle into their homeland. Even after 20 years Jacob's guilt over his shabby treatment of Esau had not completely disappeared, and the looming reunion rekindled his fear that Esau's anger had not abated. Jacob figured that the day of revenge had been only postponed, not canceled. As his unwieldy entourage made its slow and awkward way toward the hoped-for homeland, Jacob's fears escalated. Then came the report of his scouts that Esau was indeed coming to meet Jacob with 400 men. His intentions had to be evil, so Jacob sent gifts on ahead to help temper his brother's anger. He then split his family into two groups; if one group was attacked, the others could flee. At last, having done everything he could think of to prepare, he found himself alone in the night near the river Jabbok. Out of the darkness a man seemed to materialize, who, Jacob could only assume, was an enemy. The ensuing wrestling match was, I believe, completely staged by the Lord, to put Jacob to the test. As the contest continued, the Opponent finally said, "Let me go, for the day is breaking" (Gen. 32:26, RSV), suggesting that He was powerless to break free from Jacob's strength. But at a touch He put Jacob's hip out of joint, so I have to believe the outcome of the match was totally within His control. It was not a test of strength—it was a test of perseverance, of holding fast and not letting go. That was the test Jacob passed. He had been through many a trial and had finally learned that to maintain his hold on the Lord was the only solution, not only for nights of crises, but also for all the times of nagging doubts that can turn even the brightest days into dark depressions. It was a turning point that the Lord recognized, by changing his name from Jacob, the "heel gripper/opportunist," to Israel, "one who prevails with God." From that experience he went forth to meet his problems with a new assurance that God would always be there with him. His confession of years before now took on a more permanent sense: "Surely the Lord is in this place; and I did not know it." His fears of meeting his twin dissolved, for an angel had visited Esau that same night. As they came together in the morning, "Esau ran to meet him, and embraced him, and fell on his neck and kissed him, and they wept" (Gen. 33:4, RSV). It was a gripping symbol of the kind of reconciliation with both humanity and God to which the Hound of Heaven loves to call us back. In addition, through all the coming turmoil of settling into their promised land, that experience at the Jabbok and the following reunion would stand as a reminder to Jacob that, while times of darkness would come again, he should never again forget that the light of God is always close at hand. He doesn't promise to wave all the darkness away; rather, He promises to go with us into the darkness and never leave us alone. In the words of the song: "The Lord is my light . . . ; by day and by night He leads me along."

Most of Jacob's early life appears as an ongoing saga that shouts, "opportunist," "schemer," "deceiver." But, as with all biblical stories, the focus, at length, shifted from the humans involved to God. Throughout the Old Testament and into the New, God is repeatedly referred to as the God of Abraham, Isaac, and Jacob. That the God of purity and truth would so identify Himself with Jacob the deceiver, Jacob the opportunist, is at the same time shocking and encouraging. Tracking hounds are good, but the celestial Hound does much more. He not only follows us unerringly; He patiently bails us out of endless predicaments, and treats us as if we were perfect followers. But in this story He goes even further: He connects His name to the deceiver. In fact, He knowingly chooses this flawed man to be the progenitor of His favored nation. Few names, biblical or historical, would take on the kind of immortality that Jacob's changed name would enjoy. For the rest of human history his children, the children of Israel, would embody in a collective way the compassion, the patience, and the forgiving love that God showered upon the life of this unusual man.

CHAPTER 5

MOSES:
From Exile to Troublemaker

IT WAS A LARGE AND RAUCOUS FAMILY that settled into the favored spot in Egypt called the land of Goshen. They were not the kind of people who could go unnoticed. The visibility of the clan was enhanced by the prominence of their patriarch, who had not only saved his own family from the rigors of famine, but had enabled Egypt to be the supplier of grain through the famine. Hence, Joseph had become a legend among his family and among the Egyptians as well. But with famines long past, the leadership and legend of the famous Hebrew rapidly became only an interesting bit of Egyptian lore.

With the inauguration of a new pharaoh the fortunes of Joseph's family were about to plummet. As the numbers of the family rapidly increased, many of the children of Israel called to mind the earlier promises made to Abraham, Isaac, and Jacob. "Look toward heaven, and number the stars. . . . So shall your descendants be" (Gen. 15:5, RSV). "Your descendants shall be like the dust of the earth, and you shall spread . . . to the west and to the east and to the north and to the south; and by you and your descendants shall all the families of the earth [be blessed]" (Gen. 28:14, RSV). There was little doubt: the promises were beginning to come true.

But the family's growing prosperity was becoming a ruler's paranoid nightmare. The new pharaoh, "who did not know Joseph" (Ex. 1:8, RSV), did not like what he saw over in the plush meadowlands of Goshen. The Israelites' phenomenal growth triggered Egyptian panic, so Pharaoh simply seized their land and "made their lives bitter with hard service, in mortar and brick, and in all kinds of work in the field" (verse 14, RSV). The privileged status that Joseph's family had enjoyed while he lived disappeared quickly after his death. Now what was happening to the promises? Had something important in God's instruction been overlooked? The once-prosperous family of Israel now found themselves common slaves to one of the world's true despots. How quickly and completely the tables had turned.

How often the Israelites' evening discussions must have turned to the topic of the absentee God. "Where is He? If He can see us in our enslavement, why doesn't He do something?" Those promises that nations would someday "bow down to you" (Gen. 27:29, RSV) now seemed almost laughable. It happens still. Why is it that when we finally acknowledge our need of divine help the Hound of Heaven seems frequently to go into hiding? "I've prayed and prayed, but God just doesn't answer." "At first I thought I was better, but now the pain is back, and it's worse than ever."

Again and again human perception is far removed from God's reality. So it was with the Hebrew slaves. As they languished under Egyptian brutality, the God of the promises was very close at hand—so close, in fact, He was within hearing distance. "God heard their groaning, and God remembered his covenant with Abraham, with Isaac, and with Jacob. And God saw the people of Israel, and God knew their condition" (Ex. 2:24, 25, RSV). What a familiar theme—we are never really out of His sight. In story after story it is the common thread, repeated with almost tiresome frequency, perhaps because we are so prone to forget. It goes like this: The human finds herself/himself alone, away, abandoned, in a far country, separated from friends and from God, and suddenly a bush ignites, or a ram bleats, or a voice comes out of the darkness to announce that God sees and hears and knows and cares. Which is not to say that the human predicament is thereby reversed. In fact, the heavenly presence frequently allows the human problem to continue unabated, during which time faith is tested and tried so that it will grow strong. For that is the nature of a sustaining faith; it is developed and strengthened when pressed from all sides to disbelieve. Too often we are admonished with the thought that the more genuine the faith, the quicker the reward. ("As soon as I opened my eyes, the pain was gone.") But faith that seems quickly rewarded may be only an entry-level faith, inviting us to that more advanced stage that says, "The pain never left, but I will never doubt His power to heal." Or to quote Job's testimonial: "Though he slay me, yet will I trust in him" (Job 13:15). We need to hear more stories that end with "I never did find my keys [I still have cancer, my child is still paralyzed], but the lessons I have learned have taught me that I can trust God completely. Nothing can shake my faith in Him." Faith that waits and trusts with little evidence on which to rest and that brings no ready answer to our "whys" requires a maturing relationship with God, and Israel's children still had a childish relationship with Him.

In something of a contrast with previous fugitives, the developing plight of Israel's children in Egypt was not really their fault. In fact, their plight was a direct result of their rapid increase in number and prosperity. Consequently, their frustration must have escalated to a fever pitch. We humans can endure keen suffering when we realize that we brought it upon ourselves, or if we feel that there is an overarching lesson we can learn from our pain. But when the agony is not only keen but seemingly pointless, and when explanations resemble hollow ramblings, our childish faith may shrivel, and our complaints may evolve into bitterness and cynicism. Israel's children felt not only far removed from their beloved Land of Promise, but abandoned by God as well. They didn't remember that heaven and Egypt were still connected by the same ladder that had brought angels down to Jacob in a rock-strewn lonely field. Israel's problem (as is ours) was one of timing. God's deliverance comes, but rarely in the time and manner that we prefer. For reasons we cannot know, His clock and purposes are rarely synchronized with ours. It may well be that "God's purposes know no haste and no delay" (Ellen G. White, *The Desire of Ages,* p. 32), but our lives have lots of both. Year after year Israel's humiliation at the hands of Pharaoh deepened. Where was God's rescue? It would come in time—God's time, and only after a false start and more delay.

With agonizingly slow motion, Israel's deliverer comes into focus—but first as a helpless baby in a basket. He then seems to disappear. Time drags. Bloody enslavement continues. Every day Israel's children cry "Why?" but the question hangs in the air, unanswered. Years pass. Finally comes the young prince, Moses, now acting as an inept double agent, who, while being groomed for Egyptian politics, figures he can deliver his Israelite kin by an occasional clandestine murder of Egyptians, one at a time (Ex. 2:12). So one fateful day, in a remote corner, he saves an Israelite by murdering an Egyptian and hurriedly burying him. If this is Heaven's Hound, sent to rescue the suffocating Israelites, something has gone awfully wrong. Clearly this hound has to be retrained. Like Jacob of old and Abraham before that, Moses will have to make his own lonely journey before he can lead anyone else's. What is it with God and journeys to a far country? Was it only when people were traveling away from their comfort zone that God could get their undivided attention? And if in those days it was hard for God to get their attention, what must it take for Him to get ours? Bombarded as we are with the visual and noise pollutions of our age, it is amazing that He can ever break through our distraction barriers.

With the discovery of the Egyptian body in the sand, the would-be deliverer suddenly finds himself at the top of Pharaoh's most-wanted list (verse 15). And so begins Moses' long journey from his position of power and privilege to a land of sheep and a life of obscurity in Midian (verse 15). The humbling process would take four decades, the entire length of today's normal work career. When pride and self-assurance have wrapped their tentacles around us, it is no small endeavor to peel them away. For Moses, 40 years of tending small-brained, irascible sheep were needed to leech that self-importance out of his being and prepare him for the humbling, gigantic task of being God's agent for badgering into submission an egocentric pharaoh. Phase two would be no less difficult—leading an impossibly large group of fairly normal, complaining people through years of traveling conditions that would periodically turn them into a mutinous hoard of rebels. His 40-year Midian retraining class, Humility 101, was eminently successful, for as it drew to a close and the voice in the fiery bush invited Moses to resume his real calling, he is truly a different person.

Now that he is "ready" Moses wants no part of it, and his attempts to spurn God's call to battle are an intriguing litany of excuses. At first it is not clear whether his pleadings stem from humility, complacency, or genuine fear. What is clear is how much he really wants to stay in Midian. And why should he not? He is happily married, has children, is long past middle age, is comfortably situated, and is warned by God that Pharaoh will reject his offers (Ex. 3:19). Who in their right mind would say yes to such a call? So, understandably, Moses tries numerous times—vainly—to counter God's call. To each of God's invitations, the recurring phrase is the plaintive protest, "But Moses said to God. . . ." But God is not quick to accept his excuses, or ours. There is a popular notion that God's patience runs thin when humans turn Him down more than three times. But frequent excuses or fleeing fugitives have little effect on the pursuit of Heaven's Hound. His patience and persistence simply have no human counterpart. But, of course, that also describes God's grace.

Moses' first excuse, "Who am I that I should go to Pharaoh, and bring the sons of Israel out?" (Ex. 3:11, RSV) suggests that either he has forgotten all about his early years in Pharaoh's household (hardly likely), or he truly believes that, with the passage of years, his opportunity has passed. After all, he is 80 and probably feels that his leadership potential is now gone. But God responds with the promise of His presence: "I will be with you" (verse 12, RSV). Even for the fainthearted that promise should be more than enough. Of course, it is not a promise that the problems will all dissolve, but that the strength to bear them will now be more than human. Admittedly God could go it alone; and maybe that is what Moses was getting at. "God, You go ahead and start without me—You don't really need me at all." Which, of course, is true; He doesn't really need us. But apparently we need the experience of learning to cooperate with Him, so He repeatedly gives us the opportunities we need but are always trying to get out of. "I will be with you." In time Moses would come to accept that simple promise completely. At the end of his life the testimony would be given: "And there has not arisen a prophet since in Israel like Moses, whom the Lord knew face to face" (Deut. 34:10, RSV).

At this point Moses is not all that enamored of being face to face with God. His next excuse centered in a serious question: "What name can I give you when the Egyptians ask who sent me?" (see Ex. 3:13). In those days a name, whether of human being or god, would include something of the character of the being. It would be more than a little pretentious for Moses to come in his own authority before Pharaoh and make demands. But if he came representing a deity, that deity must at least have a name.

The name God gives him is very strange. It is built upon a form of the verb "to be." In effect God says, "I am the Being One," or "I am the One who is. Tell the Egyptians, 'The Being One has sent me'" (see verse 14). The Egyptians had a variety of gods, all of which had names of one kind or another, but the names all constituted various kinds of limitations. If a god's domain was in the sun or in the water, or over the crops, much of the mystery of that god was diminished. But the God Moses is told to introduce to the Egyptians is to be announced as the "Being One," which stresses His fullness and His mystery. It is not terribly surprising, then, that Moses objects by asserting that the Egyptians, whose gods had specific names and specific domains of power, simply won't believe him or his God of mystery. Whereupon, God directs him, in a series of physical phenomena such as rod-throwing and serpent-catching, while acknowledging that the Egyptians will not be impressed. Not surprisingly, Moses keeps groping for reasons to say no. This time he pleads that he is too "slow of speech and tongue" to go as a spokesman to the powerful ruler of Egypt (Ex. 4:10, RSV). But God counters that He alone is the creator of a person's mouth, so He can certainly put words into it if that becomes necessary. At length, all his excuses expended, Moses simply whimpers, "Oh, my Lord, send . . . some other person" (verse 13, RSV). Clearly he would rather wander the fields with stubborn sheep than return to arguing with stubborn people.

So God counters his last objection by saying, "Fine, take your thick tongue and tell your brother, Aaron, all about our little dialogue. Tell him that you are both going to Egypt. You will be My primary representative, and Aaron will be your spokesman and interpreter, and as I promised you, I will go with you" (see verses 14-16). End of discussion. At last, after many vigorous protests, Moses capitulates. The Hound has again demonstrated His tireless pursuit, and the fugitive has run out of reasons to flee. Not that his struggles have ended. To a great degree, his toughest tests are about to begin. How frequently it happens: God perseveres and gets our attention; we turn back toward Him, only to experience shattering problems and repeated attacks on our newfound faith. The attacks on Moses' faith were about to begin in earnest.

Moses' first appeal to Pharaoh to let the people go had a very unfortunate result. Pharaoh, fearing that Moses' reappearance will awaken ideas of freedom in the slaves' minds, decides to make their lives more difficult. To remind them forcefully that any ideas of freedom are premature,

Pharaoh reduces their supply of straw but maintains the same quota of bricks, thereby giving them less time to sit and plan any kind of insurrection mischief. "Let heavier work be laid on them; then they will labor at it and pay no attention to deceptive words" (Ex. 5:9, NRSV). Whereupon, the Israelites complain bitterly to Moses that, thanks to him, they not only have not been delivered, but now their lot has become much worse than before. Some deliverer he turned out to be! Forty years before, he had done it all wrong, and now it appears to the Hebrews that he is picking up right where he had left off—only this time it's worse. Now they are all suffering as a result of his inept attempts to deliver them. They appear ready to run him back to Midian, if they could. Since he doesn't seem about to leave, they give him a vote of no confidence. "You have brought us into bad odor with Pharaoh and his officials, and have put a sword in their hand to kill us" (verse 21, NRSV).

Nothing is working out right for Moses or for the Israelites—but, of course, that was Moses' fear back in Midian and was the reason for his many attempts to escape God's invitation. So Moses' renewed relationship with God turns into impassioned complaints—complaints about God's treatment of Israel and a repeat of the wish that he was still in Midian. "O Lord, why have you mistreated this people? Why did you ever send me? Since I first came to Pharaoh to speak in your name, he has mistreated this people, and you have done nothing at all to deliver your people" (verses 22, 23, NRSV). He seems to say, "I've done my part, and it has only gotten me in trouble with Pharaoh and with the people because You haven't done Yours. You said You would be with me, but so far I haven't seen much evidence of Your presence. And Pharaoh sure hasn't either, or he wouldn't be so arrogant. Please, Lord, what more can I do? I've told him what You said to tell him, and we're all still here. Did I miss something?"

What a common frustration that is. We are confronted with a difficult situation. After fretful discussions with family and/or friends, we finally turn to God. If He seems to answer, we may attempt to follow His direction, only to see nothing change. But a week/month/year later we have one of those amazing "aha" moments and realize that the real problem was not God's answer but His timing. Our moment-to-moment time frame often merges awkwardly, if at all, with God's plans. How often He must want to caution us as He did Habakkuk: "If it seem slow, wait for it; it will surely come" (Hab. 2:3, RSV).

And so the plagues begin, but the result is far different than Moses had expected. Even though the Lord had warned him that Pharaoh would be quite stubborn, when the spectacular displays of God's power in nature began Moses must have believed that Pharaoh would quickly capitulate. But before the victory of deliverance, faith and endurance would be severely tested. It seems to be a thing with God. He pushes our faith and trust to the very brink, not just to watch us struggle with our stress, but to make the deliverance that much more memorable. A victory easily won is easily forgotten. The victory of Israel over Egypt is celebrated still.

Clearly the emotional buildup was enormous. As the plagues come and go and Pharaoh waffles again and again, it is hard even to imagine the anger all the people must have heaped upon Moses. The Egyptian people loathed him as the renegade former prince who had returned to devastate their lives and land with the plagues. And while the Israelites weren't touched by most of the plagues, they were close enough to see and hear the results. Consequently, as their hopes were raised and then dashed again and again, they must have come to despise Moses as the greatest purveyor of false hope in all their tortured history. Moses' experience was turning out even worse than his pessimistic predictions.

It is easy for us to sympathize with Moses' and the Hebrews' frustration. After all, what are we to make of the agonizing delay of the deliverance? And what are we to make of the fact that of the 14 references to Pharaoh's heart being "hardened," seven of those references say that the Lord was the one who hardened Pharaoh's heart? What is the meaning of this cat-and-mouse game in which the cat seems to be manipulating the mouse? Is Pharaoh freely making his own bad decisions, or is he a helpless pawn, oblivious to the part he is acting out on God's great stage? Before the drama began, God warned Moses "that the king of Egypt will not let you go unless compelled by a mighty hand. So I will stretch out my hand and smite Egypt with all the wonders . . . ; after that he will let you go" (Ex. 3:19, 20, RSV). That statement, coupled with references that Pharaoh hardened his own heart (e.g., Ex. 8:15, 32; 9:34), puts the decision-making in Pharaoh's hand. So either there is a contradiction in the terms, or else God's hardening should not be viewed as usurping Pharaoh's freedom of choice. Perhaps we should view God's "hardening" not as a direct action on Pharaoh's heart, but as the indirect result of his repeated refusal to respond to God's directive. In that sense, each refusal makes him a little more determined to refuse again. Each invitation presents him with another "hardening" opportunity.

Meanwhile, Moses is experiencing a different kind of hardening. His weekly futile confrontations with Pharaoh are building in him a steely persistence that will help him weather the withering attacks he will receive from his own people when they realize they have given up the tasty leeks of Goshen for that boring wilderness fare called manna (Num. 11:5, 6). Moses' training, begun in Midian, isn't quite finished yet. But at the time, all he knew was that he was enduring a weekly humiliation. His dire warning, followed by the shock value of a devastating plague, produced only a short-term-trembling pharaoh followed by a quick reversal. Another threat followed, and then the whole cycle would be repeated. Would the humiliation never end?

Ultimately, of course, Pharaoh lost. Through the plagues he lost his land and his firstborn son. And through his last vain attempt to recapture his slaves, he probably lost his life. It was a sad chapter in Egyptian history, all record of which was kept out of official documents. But if the Egyptian record keepers thought they had covered up the humiliating incident by keeping it out of their historical documents, they could hardly have been more wrong. There was a heavenly record keeper who saw to it that, for the rest of time, people would read and reread the account of Egyptian arrogance and of the God of power who humbled a powerful king.

Through it all, Moses, a man who in his youth was primed to be one of God's greatest servant/leaders, became instead one of the more spectacular fugitives first. Having been adopted into the Egyptian royal household, he gradually lost touch with the God of his heritage. He didn't completely forget his God; he just lost touch with how to trust in Him. It's a common occurrence. The pace and pressure around us consume our time and energy. We engage ourselves in no bad causes, only engrossing ones—like careers and house payments and fitness and even church activities. We certainly don't forget God; we just gradually lose touch with how to trust in Him. So when extreme circumstances crop up, we, like Moses, resort to the resources we know best—our own ingenuity and astuteness and perseverance. Then, when all else fails, we finally respond to that insistent voice and try to get back in touch with Him.

When Moses tapped into his own resources of shrewdness and cunning, it simply resulted in futile violence, which in turn led to his unfortunate flight from his God-intended post of duty. The detour lasted for the greater part of his adult life. Getting back in touch with God took time and a radical change in surroundings. His time spent drifting away from God brought with it a heavy toll. Had he kept firm hold of the God of his birth, had he daily taken the time to "be still, and know that I am God" (Ps. 46:10), might the enslavement of Israel been shortened some 40 years? Was Moses' youthful arrogance partly to blame for the length of Israel's years of terrible oppression? One thing is clear: his bravado made him a fugitive in a far-off land, where, in time, the Hound of Heaven would hunt him down and mysteriously but insistently call him back to the mission God had intended all along.

By the time Pharaoh's knees finally buckled and Moses and his people were able to escape the king's clutches, Moses had grown into that stalwart leader of faith who would cling to God through decades of pressure that would surely have crushed a lesser person. When he was being put to his first incredible post-Exodus test and Pharaoh's armies were storming up from the rear, the now-mature man of God boldly badgered the people's shaky faith by throwing down the challenge "Fear not, stand firm, and see the salvation of the Lord, which he will work for you today; for the Egyptians whom you see today, you shall never see again. The Lord will fight for you, and you have only to be still" (Ex. 14:13, 14, RSV).

"You have only to be still." What a promise. What a statement of faith. Surely a man of such faith could never lapse. But the life of faith should not be thought seamless or as an all-or-nothing kind of experience. Moses had matured into a completely committed, trusting servant of the Most High. But human character will always need to pray with honesty, "Forgive us our debts." While there is scant biblical support for the notion of "once saved, always saved," some views of perfectionism come uncomfortably close to that mistaken concept. The idea is widespread that Christians on the sanctification road must arrive soon at that coveted destination where "not even by a thought" do they transgress. However, that notion is weakened by the fact that outside of the very truncated story of Enoch, we can find no biblical example that such a saint has ever lived. At least it wasn't Moses. Late in his experience of leading Israel, Moses had that brief lapse that, in his view, cost him dearly. After all he had been through, he was denied entrance into Canaan with those for whom he had poured out his life. By human standards the penalty seemed to exceed the crime. Hassled incessantly by whiners with extremely short-term and selective memories, they have once again run short of water and patience, and look back with warped longing for the "comforts" of the slave camps. "Why have you made us come up out of Egypt, to bring us to this evil place?" (Num. 20:5, RSV). As with their first water shortage just after the Red Sea deliverance, when a large threat diminishes they quickly focus on the smaller discomforts and magnify them. Past miracles are quickly forgotten in the face of immediate discomfort. How exasperating. How normal! How many worry trips have we taken right on the heels of some notable answer to prayer? "Lord, I just don't see how I can make it through this week, given what I face at work." And He might respond, "But remember two weeks ago, when that deadline seemed impossible to meet, and then it was mysteriously extended for two more days? Have you forgotten so quickly?"

As he has done so many times before, Moses takes his exasperation to the Lord, who patiently explains how He will once again intercede. God's instruction is very clear, calm, and deliberate, and not really open to misunderstanding: "Tell the rock . . . to yield its water" (verse 8, RSV). But with his patience stretched to the breaking point, Moses presumes upon his close relationship with God and speaks as if he and God have collaborated and together they have decided to capitulate to this bunch of ungrateful wretches. "Hear now, you rebels; shall we bring forth water for you out of this rock?" (verse 10, RSV). Whack! And he smacks the rock with his ever-present rod, and the water gushes out. "Shall *we* bring forth water for you?" "Moses, have you suddenly become executive assistant to God with decision-making authority?" His impatience was understandable, but not his failure to follow God's clear instruction. But it was his failure to "believe in me" and "to sanctify me in the eyes of the people" (verse 12, RSV) that God reproves. It was a brief but all-important lapse. After the numberless times that Moses had come crawling to God, having fallen speechless and helpless before some humanly impossible situation, it was surely arrogant for him to hoist himself onto the podium with God and claim even a pinch of the glory for himself. *We* can never get water or anything else from a rock. On the other hand, God, all by Himself, can turn a rock into a well, water into wine, and any number of spectacular wonders. Over all our achievements, large or small, must hang that all-important confession "For *thine* is the kingdom and the power."

"So Moses the servant of the Lord died there in the land of Moab. . . . And the people of Israel wept for Moses" (Deut. 34:5-8, RSV). What a journey! From the royal court of Pharaoh to a distant land of hiding, back to Pharaoh, then back to a wilderness journey that ended just short of his destination. His journey back to God had begun with that strange invitation from a bush where Moses "was afraid to look at God" (Ex. 3:6, RSV) and in fact wasn't real sure what to call Him (verse 13). It ended with some of the most glowing testimonials in Scripture. "And there has not arisen a prophet since in Israel like Moses, whom the Lord knew face to face, none like him for all the signs and the wonders which the Lord sent him to do in the land of Egypt, . . . and for all the mighty power and all the great and terrible deeds which Moses wrought in the sight of all Israel" (Deut. 34:10-12, RSV).

And that's not all. Centuries later, when the author of Hebrews listed the heroes of faith in chapter 11, Moses, the one-time fugitive, is remembered only for his faith, not at all for his various departures from the path of faith. "By faith he left Egypt, not being afraid of the anger of the king; for he endured as seeing him who is invisible" (verse 27, RSV). But the last reference is perhaps the most surprising of all. It seems that God's archangel, Michael, had marked the spot of that lonely burial and, over the protestations of the devil himself, came and claimed the body (Jude 9). So while he was denied entrance to Canaan, God rewarded him with a grander entrance—to that "city which has foundations, whose builder and maker is God" (verse 10, RSV). What a journey! What a life! What a God!

CHAPTER 6

SAMSON:

From Strength to Weakness

AT TIMES IT'S HARD TO TELL GOD'S HEROES from His fugitives. Samson certainly blurs the distinction. As the curtain lifts, the stage is set for heroism; but what follows are a series of exploits characterized by fights and flights, battling hero and running fugitive. But we must let the story unfold more slowly.

At the start the author packs into one verse 40 years of Israelite waywardness and Philistine oppression. "And the people of Israel again did what was evil in the sight of the Lord; and the Lord gave them into the hand of the Philistines for forty years" (Judges 13:1, RSV). But in the very next verse he alters his style and begins, ever so slowly, to spell out in minute detail the beginning of the Israelite solution. As He has done on numerous occasions (Sarah: Gen. 16:1; Rebekah: Gen. 25:21; Rachel: Gen. 30:1, 2; Hannah: 1 Sam. 1), God begins with a "barren" woman. What is it with God and all these childless women? He seems to delight in reducing human resources to their absolute minimum so as to emphasize, for our weak faith, the ease with which He can reverse the odds. Who but God would repeatedly begin stories of large families with infertile couples?

The birth announcement, like the story to follow, is stranger than fiction. An angel in the guise of a man appears twice to the woman to announce her pregnancy before appearing to her husband, Manoah. This approach reverses the order of the Abraham/Sarah dialogues, in which the divine visitor appeared repeatedly to Abraham without saying anything to Sarah. Given the male-dominant culture, it is not surprising that Manoah is miffed and wants to get the message firsthand, rather than translated through his wife. Consequently he implores the Lord that the man/angel might come to them again and "teach us [translate: "me"] what we are to do concerning the boy" (Judges 13:8, NRSV). Since the messenger had been quite explicit with Manoah's wife, he didn't feel the need to repeat everything just to satisfy Manoah, but simply added the admonition that his wife should "give heed to all that I said to her" (verse 13, NRSV). It was going against the grain of the culture for a husband to be told, "Your wife will explain it to you." But then again, if God didn't frequently do the unconventional and prick the conscience of culture, our world would be even more pathetically adrift than it is.

What the angel had told "the woman" (verse 3; strangely, her name is not given) was that she would bear a son and he would be a Nazirite—a truly sobering announcement. That term does not relate to the city of Nazareth, but comes from the Hebrew word meaning "one consecrated" or "one separated," and meant that the person was to be set apart to God in a very special way. Dedication of a babe in arms is one of the pleasant religious rituals we continue to practice. The new parents, hopeful and responsive, are challenged to provide a spiritually rich environment for the growing child. The surrounding community of faith is attentive and supportive; terms like *hopes* and *dreams* are prominent, and prayer for the parents and baby is fervent. The little ones are touched and held by the officiating ministers, and gifts often mark the occasion to serve as reminders of that very special service.

But dedication of a Nazirite went further. Often it involved some sacred cause or vow, but it could also mean a special calling as a holy warrior. "War in early Israel was a holy enterprise, and while on active duty the warrior was in a state of sanctity" (J. C. Rylaarsdam, "Nazirite," *The Interpreter's Dictionary of the Bible* [Nashville: Abingdon Press, 1962], vol. 3, p. 526). This aspect would rise to prominence as Samson's story developed. The Nazirite vow could be taken by either a man or a woman, or by a parent for a child, as in Samson's case. It could be taken for a specified time period (Num. 6:13) or for a lifetime (Judges 13:5). The person dedicated was not to eat or drink anything from the grapevine, was not to eat anything unclean, was not to go near a dead body, and was not to cut her/his hair. Clearly it was not a commitment for the faint of heart. Nor would a parent enter lightly into such dedication of a child. No doubt that was the reason Manoah asked twice for clarification: "What is to be the boy's rule of life; what is he to do?" (verse 12, NRSV; see also verse 8). It had been made very plain to his wife, but Manoah is clearly apprehensive about such an assignment and wants to hear it firsthand. In fact, one could get the feeling that Manoah was getting cold feet about having a son if he was to be saddled with this list of restrictions. Child rearing is tough enough with just the normal prohibitions; add-ons would only make it worse. Actually, the list of don'ts was not that long, but if Manoah knew anything about human nature, he surely suspected that one day young Samson would come running home, wanting nothing more than a drink of grape juice and a haircut! "Really, Angel, are you absolutely sure? Past heroes such as Abraham, Isaac, and Jacob did great things for God, and they never took the vow. Why can't Samson be like one of them? That would be enough commitment for us."

But it is not with us to choose the price of parenthood. The wonders of today's genetic engineering have brought with them a questionable sense of control over virtually all aspects of the reproductive process. In fact, an attitude not far removed from consumerism has crept ever closer to the bearing of children. In vitro fertilization, sonograms, sex selection, and surrogate mothering are only a few of the practices that have contributed to the notion that childbearing is now something that can be under our complete control. There need be no surprises. Which can lull parents into the illusion that child rearing, like childbearing, need not involve sacrifice. Admittedly the price for Manoah and wife of rearing Samson would turn out to be far higher than normal. But the lesson of sacrifice should not be lost on today's parents. Unlike Samson, our children may drink all the grape juice they want and may freely choose short hair, but in lots of other ways the physical and emotional price of supporting them from crib to college can be staggering nonetheless. What parent has not, at some point or many points, wanted to say, with Manoah, "O, Lord . . . teach us what we are to do with the boy" (verse 8, RSV)? "Lord, we've tried everything and nothing seems to work; what do You suggest?"

As the birth announcement ended, Manoah and wife have the unnerving sense that they are in the presence of the supernatural. Groping for some sense of control, Manoah asks the stranger his name, for it was felt that to know a person's name was to have a measure of control over the situation or the person (cf. Ex. 3:13, 14). The angel replied with a question of his own: "Why do you ask my name, seeing it is wonderful?" (Judges 13:18, RSV). Was he referring to his name, or to the events surrounding the announcement? Who can say? Wanting to demonstrate a gesture of hospitality, Manoah offers the visitor food, but he declines, suggesting instead that Manoah offer a sacrifice to God. Then to add awe to the spectacle, the "man" disappears in the flames of the sacrifice. God can show Hollywood a thing or two about special effects. Manoah and wife are dumbstruck and fall to the ground in worship and fear, with Manoah blurting out that they are about to die. His wife, the more rational of the two, reasons that if the Lord was out to kill them, He would hardly have made all those wonderful promises about a coming baby!

As quiet descends upon them, their questions come back into focus. What does it all mean? What kind of birth and childhood await us? "Lord, could You just fill us in a bit more?" But if further instructions were given, we know nothing of them. In keeping with the biblical descriptions of child rearing, the birth and childhood of Samson are compacted into one verse: "And the woman bore a son, and called his name Samson; and the boy grew, and the Lord blessed him" (verse 24, RSV). In the next verse he is a young man ready to start his God-ordained calling, being stirred by the Spirit of the Lord. But the parent-child interactions are left out. Did the parents spoil their only child? Were they overly protective of their miracle boy, the child of "barrenness"? Did it become commonplace for him to get his way? In any case, the stage is set for some of the most fascinating war stories of all time. The fantastic and larger-than-life Rambo/terminator stories of movie fame could have taken their script from these tales of the solitary hero who would go up against an army and, against impossible odds, consistently come out the winner.

In spite of the Spirit's stirring, before he even starts down the path of God's call he wanders off into some pretty thick brambles. You don't go far into the story before you get the feeling that this young man is going to give the Hound of Heaven a run for His money. "I saw one of the daughters of the Philistines at Timnah and I want to marry her," he tells his parents (see Judges 14:2). It is infatuation at first sight. Since his boyhood years are hidden from us, we can only jump to the conclusion that such a request hit his folks like a thunderclap. At the same time, if we could peel back the covering of that one terse verse that refers to his birth and growth (Judges 13:24), we might see hints that the traits of headstrong arrogance had been gestating for years. If so, his parents may not have been completely dumbstruck at his self-serving request. But whether or not they were surprised by it, they clearly disagreed with it and tried to reason him out of it and redirect his ardor toward a nice Jewish girl. But he would have none of it. "Get her for me; for she pleases me well" (Judges 14:3, RSV).

There is the suggestion that it was all a clever ruse on his part; that marrying a Philistine girl was all part of his master plot to harass and ultimately defeat the Philistines, "for he was seeking an occasion against the Philistines" (verse 4, RSV). But if the hoped-for marriage was all part of a devious anti-Philistine plan, Samson bungled it badly. Before the marriage was a week old his lovely new wife betrayed him. On the way to his first formal date with the Philistine beauty, he had killed a lion with his bare hands. Then later, on his way to the rehearsal dinner (to his later regret, he didn't spend much time getting acquainted with his fiancé), he discovered that bees had built a honeycomb in the carcass of the lion. From that he concocted a riddle to tell at his wedding reception in hopes of stumping and humiliating his new wife's countrymen. It went like this: "Out of the eater came something to eat. Out of the strong came something sweet" (verse 14, RSV). If they could solve it in seven days, he would give them 30 suits of clothes. If they failed, they would have to give him 30 suits of clothes. But it backfired when, after her countrymen pressured her, she finally was able to wheedle the answer out of Samson and pass it along, to the great delight of the opponents. Just what kind of bride was he getting? Clearly it was not going to be a marriage made in heaven.

His fury at being outwitted was instantaneous. He stalked out of the wedding celebrations and immediately collected the 30 suits, and he saw to it that they all came off the backs of Philistines, all of whom died in the transaction. When it was all over, he was still "in hot anger." And then it got worse. He had left the wedding celebration in such a hurry and was gone so long that the bride's father gave her to the best man, in the absence of the hotheaded Israelite groom. This only escalated

Samson's anger. So this time he decided to destroy their food source. He caught 300 foxes. Three hundred foxes! How do you catch one fox? How did he catch 300? Then he figured a way to turn them into firebrands, and turned them loose in the grainfields and olive orchards of the Philistines. It had a devastating effect.

But violence breeds escalating violence, so when the Philistines found out who had destroyed their fields, they seized Samson's new wife and her father and killed them both. Whereupon Samson returned the violence "with great slaughter" (Judges 15:8, RSV), following which he went into hiding. But his frequent flare-ups were having all the wrong effect. The Philistines were the occupying force, so their reprisals were felt not only by Samson but by the people of Judah, who were not at all interested in a guerrilla war, or in any other kind of war that would cost them anything. It appears they would rather continue to suffer under the oppressive hand of the Philistines than make any sacrifices. So a delegation of some 3,000 of them sought out Samson in his hiding place with the question "What then is this that you have done to us?" (verse 11, RSV). His petulant response came off sounding self-serving, if not childish: "As they did to me, so have I done to them." So the men of Judah wimped out and pleaded with Samson to let them hand him over to the Philistines. Having seen his previous amazing exploits, they felt certain that he could easily escape his captors. But by handing him over, the men of Judah would demonstrate that the animosity was between Samson and the Philistines, and therefore the Philistines would direct their reprisals against only Samson, and spare the larger community of Judah. They no doubt realized that they couldn't end all the violence, but perhaps they could end the violence against them. However, their concept of "peace at any price" would not set well with the people, and it wouldn't set at all well with Samson. But to give an impression of cooperation, Samson allowed the men of Judah to tie him up and begin the handover procedure. When the Philistines came to complete the transaction, however, a surge of power came over him. Instead of surrendering to his captors, he amazingly converted a donkey jawbone into a deadly weapon and single-handedly wiped out a 1,000-man platoon (verse 15).

God's warriors come in a dizzying array of colors and talents. At times it is difficult to determine where God's divine intervention ends and human vengeance or ambition begins. But throughout Samson's escapades of bloodletting it appears that his Lord was never very far away—even in those times when he seemed to be acting pretty much on his own. But it is when humans stray that the Hound of Heaven does His best work. Did Samson launch out on his own in this episode of carnage, or was he God's tool of judgment for a thousand godless Philistines? Samson makes a passing reference to God's help: "Thou hast granted this great deliverance by the hand of thy servant" (verse 18, RSV). It is one of the few reflective moments in the story, and it is in the midst of a desperate appeal for a drink ("Shall I now die of thirst?"). No doubt the killing of a thousand men could cause quite a thirst to develop, but was he really about to die of thirst? Or was this Samson's typical way of demanding that his wants be met? Similar, for example, to his earlier appeal to his parents: "Get her for me; for she pleases me well" (Judges 14:3, RSV).

Once again the God who condescends to human wishes and weaknesses patiently responds to Samson's plea and miraculously provides water from a "hollow place" (Judges 15:19). So why is God so willing to cater to the whims of such a headstrong, violent man? Surely there have been more deserving children of God who, in desperate straits, could have benefited from such divine intervention, yet they languished or died alone, seemingly abandoned. It is one of those questions that leaps to mind, but no answer follows. The inexplicable confronts us again and again. The murderous, adulterous David is blessed and rewarded, while the faithful Jeremiah seems to live an extended martyrdom and dies alone. Jesus goes about healing and even raising the dead, while faithful John the Baptist wonders why he has been abandoned to suffer and die. So Samson gets thirsty, and God creates an artesian well just for him and he is thereby "revived" (verse 19). At times God steps in, and at times He steps back. But to ponder too long on the question of why often gives rise only to a stymied mind and a waning faith. God has His reasons, which our reason cannot know. That is when faith takes on its deepest meaning.

One thing becomes clear: whether Samson was running away from God or running back to God or running with God, he was never far from God. This time a private drinking fountain revived Samson, but revived him to do what work for God? The author of the account simply collapses 20 years of Samson's contributions into one brief phrase: "He judged Israel in the days of the Philistines twenty years" (verse 20). It is one of the few positive comments about Samson's work—and we don't really know what it meant.

In the next verse (Judges 16:1) the author again slows his style and proceeds to give a detailed account of another incident that makes us wonder about this strange man. The combination of strength and weakness in the same person is rarely set out as blatantly as it is in Samson. Here in Gaza, when he is trapped by his enemies, he rises in the dark of night, breaks loose the whole city gate, and carries it away as he makes his escape. But his demonstration of superhuman strength is part and parcel of his sexual liaison with a harlot. It raises the often-troubling issue of the extent of God's involvement, cooperation with, and even empowerment of an overt sinner, not an accidental or struggling sinner. We generally take a dim view of the thought that God cooperates with people who practice questionable lifestyles. We readily acknowledge that God forgives all manner of bad living, and only then condescends to fill the cleaned-up person with the power of His Spirit. But Samson seems to have God's help and power in the very midst of his ongoing sinful practices. Sometimes we have cautioned young people about the dangers of certain questionable activities by suggesting that their protecting angels just might abandon them if they go where they shouldn't. Samson's Gaza incident doesn't seem to support that notion. If God left him when he went to the brothel, He certainly seems to have been waiting patiently for him at the door when he left. Perhaps the best we can say is that while God never approves of sinful behavior, He does not withdraw His power or His presence from sinning humans. This is not at all to say that He trivializes sin; rather, His involvement with sinning humans is much more patient and complex than humans can grasp. "For my thoughts are not your thoughts, neither are your ways my ways, says the Lord. For as the heavens are higher than the earth, so are my ways higher than your ways and my thoughts than your thoughts" (Isa. 55:8, 9, RSV). It is when we have strayed the farthest that Heaven's Hound is most needed.

Samson's last episode with a woman is perhaps the saddest. The first woman "pleased him" (see Judges 14:3); others probably satisfied him, but Delilah he loved (Judges 16:4). Sadly, her feelings for him were for sale. When the Philistine lords offered her money to betray him, there is not a hint of hesitation on her part. As this last relationship plays out, Samson appears to take seriously the meaning of his parents' early vows for him. Three times he can't bring himself to reveal the reason for his long hair. Was he trying to protect the importance of his God-ordained mission, or just playing games with the Philistines at the expense of his lover? Or had he come to believe that his unusual strength was really his own? It would be an easy pit to fall into. Throughout his incredible exploits thus far, the only time he appeared to commune with God was when he needed a drink. His prayer life appears pretty well nonexistent. If he had in fact drifted away from the God of his youth, it is just as likely that he had come to view his long-ago vow as something now detached from his day-to-day life. Still, in those rare, quiet moments, when Samson took time to reflect, he knew the real source of his strength.

The strength of the tempter must not be underestimated. "And when she pressed him hard with her words day after day, and urged him," "he told her all his mind" (verse 16, RSV). The tempter doesn't just come with a casual suggestion and then, at our first rebuff, slink away silently to sit and sulk. "She pressed him hard . . . day after day, and urged him." Patient persistence is a prime ingredient of temptation. Without the Lord's help, it is a one-sided battle that we can only lose. "He told her all his mind, and said to her, 'I have been a Nazirite to God from my mother's womb. If I be shaved, then my strength will leave me, and I shall become weak . . . like any other man'" (verse 17, RSV). Three times he had lied about the source of his strength, and three times she had called in the Philistines to seize him. When she pressed him this fourth time, did he not suspect that she just might call them again? Is Samson so besotted with Delilah that he will sacrifice his very life to please her? So why did he reveal his deep secret unless he believed that God would come to his rescue no matter what? If he revealed it because he thought Delilah would keep his secret, then he deserved to have a surprising wake-up call. "And she said, 'The Philistines are upon you, Samson!' And he awoke from his sleep, and said, 'I will go out as at other times, and shake myself free.' And he did not know that the Lord had left him. And the Philistines seized him and gouged out his eyes, and brought him down to Gaza, and bound him with bronze fetters; and he ground at the mill in the prison" (verses 20-22, RSV). This time the

Lord could not ignore Samson's apparent disdain for his Nazirite vow. There are limits to God's forbearance. As we have seen, He sometimes steps in and sometimes steps back. This time He stepped back, because it was the only way a lesson could be learned and passed on to us. Also, if there is one constant through all God's mysterious actions, it is the theme called "redemptive." Even now He is not through with the wayward Samson. But for now Samson has to go it alone, and when he is alone, he is pretty pathetic. Mutilated, stripped of strength and dignity, he now strikingly resembles an animal. And so Samson, a man with spectacular promise, decided early on to go his own way. Violently he made good on his ill-conceived wagers, returning evil for evil, wreaking havoc upon the enemy's lives and crops, but trivializing the real mission God had planned for him. Heaven's Hound was kept very busy throughout the entire life of this tragic hero/fugitive.

The final episode, like all the others, was characterized by tragedy. On the occasion of a grand Philistine festival of sacrifice to their god Dagon, as their alcohol took effect, someone began to chant for Samson. Since he had been their sworn enemy for years, it was only fitting that they should now reap the sweet rewards of vengeance. Whereupon, they brought out Samson to serve as a kind of court jester, "that he may make sport for us" (verse 25, RSV). It was the ultimate humiliation. His first encounter with the Philistines had humiliated him, and now it was happening again. But he was to have the final word.

It was not just that his hair was growing back. He had recently had lots of time to reflect on his life and his choices. Those troubled thoughts brought him little comfort and much regret. They also brought him back to his senses and to his God, who welcomed him back. Perhaps he finally realized that his role as God's warrior had missed the mark by a wide margin. Though he couldn't know what would be written about him, he must have known, as we know now, that the highlights of his 20 years of leadership, those events that alone would be remembered to the end of time, would be two betrayals by two different women, several murderous rampages, a pyrotechnic display that destroyed crops, an incident with a harlot, and a death by suicide. It was less than an impressive legacy. He had reached the bottom.

But from the bottom the only real view is up, and Samson began to look up. At the same time, his prayer for vengeance ("that I may be avenged upon the Philistines" [verse 28, RSV]) is hardly a noble prayer. He did not, like Stephen (Acts 7:59, 60) and Jesus (Luke 23:34), pray for his enemies to be forgiven. But he did acknowledge that God was the source of his life and strength. "O Lord God, remember me, I pray thee, and strengthen me" (Judges 16:28). Given his role as God's warrior, perhaps the most we should expect is this heartfelt cry that his final sacrifice would mesh with the will of God. The Philistines had placed him between great weight-bearing pillars, and his prayer brought one final display of human effort and divine power. And somehow, in ways far beyond the reach of our meager understanding, Samson died as God's hero. The author of Hebrews includes him among those who, "through faith, conquered kingdoms . . . stopped the mouths of lions . . . won strength out of weakness, became mighty in war, put foreign armies to flight" (Heb. 11:33, 34, RSV).

Where the renegade melds into the hero is not always easy to determine. The torturous trail of Samson's life from frequent fugitive to final sacrificial hero says more eloquently than any words that there really is a "wideness in God's mercy, like the wideness of the sea."

CHAPTER 7

DAVID AND BATHSHEBA:
The Wandering King Is Found

AMONG JEWS, ANCIENT AND MODERN, no biblical character achieved an eminence closer to that of the Messiah than David. In fact, his name became a symbol for the Messiah. When the people reached a peak of messianic fervor and excitement, and anticipated the greatest of messianic demonstrations, the term that burst spontaneously from their mouths was "Hosanna to the Son of David" (Matt. 21:15). The son of *David?* They could have linked Jesus to any number of luminous ancestors. Why not Abraham or Isaac or Joseph? But the only one to whom they consistently link Him is David. This David must have been a spiritual giant. So by what stretch of imagination does he appear here among a list of "fugitives"? The answer requires a careful look at an intriguing life.

He first appears as a mere shepherd lad, the youngest of eight sons (1 Sam. 17:12). At that point, his main task was to keep close tabs on the sheep and stay out from underfoot, especially when company came. At least when prophet Samuel came to look over the family and learn about the sons, nobody even thought about David. After the seven older siblings paraded before Samuel, the prophet had to ask Jesse, "Are all your sons here?" (1 Sam. 16:11, RSV). Jesse answered, "There remains yet the youngest, but behold, he is keeping the sheep." It's almost as if Jesse is saying, "Well, now that you mention it, there is one more, but he's just a kid, and he's out looking after the sheep. You won't be interested in him." With little David, out of sight is out of mind. When David comes in from the field, the writer slows his writing style and fixes his attention and ours on the appearance of this young man, something the Lord had just told Samuel not to do. The caution about good looks was very clear: "For the Lord sees not as man sees; man looks on the outward appearance, but the Lord looks on the heart" (verse 7, RSV). Yet when David stands before him, the prophet can't help being struck by and then describing his appearance. "Now he was ruddy, and had beautiful eyes, and was handsome" (verse 12, RSV). Most of us would settle for just one or maybe two nice comments on our physical features, but the writer seems quite taken by David's appearance. He not only has rosy cheeks and beautiful eyes; he is just plain handsome. The rest of the family probably hadn't noticed, because siblings and parents usually spend so much time observing and correcting the flaws they see that they rarely notice, let alone compliment, the attractive features. So it must have come as quite a shock when Samuel got out his horn of oil and proceeded to anoint David the child as David the next king—though much time would pass before he would actually take the throne.

After the anointing, the prophet left, and presumably, David went back out to pasture, thinking, *I wonder what that was all about.* His brothers no doubt leaped to conclusions of their own, such as "That Samuel is one senile old prophet. Can you imagine a more unlikely candidate for king than little stone-throwing, psalm-singing, sheepherding David? Why doesn't God pick a new prophet when the old ones like Samuel get daffy?" Of course, we are hardly guiltless of similar misperceptions. Like David's brothers, we are frequently seized by a rush to judgment. "Lord, it's true our church/school/conference needed new leadership, but what were You thinking when You sent us this 'unusual' person to lead us? Almost the entire board agrees that it's just a bad fit. We needed a new face, but not this one." "Lord, You made it possible for us to move here and take this job, and now everything is falling apart. In fact, it looks as though I'm going to lose the very job I came here for. Why have You done this to us?" "A shepherd boy to lead a nation?"

The next incident of interest took place when David served as errand boy to his three older brothers. Eliab, Abinadab, and Shammah had gone off to war, and father Jesse began to grow worried. The battleground was probably only some 15 or 20 miles away, but given their transportation system, it was a good day's travel. So the concerned father sent his youngest to deliver some granola and cheese sandwiches ("roasted grain" and "ten loaves of bread" and "ten cheeses," according to 1 Samuel 17:17, 18, NIV), and then bring him word on their well-being.

David's visit to the army camp brought more than a few surprises. First, he surprised his brothers, who were not overjoyed to see him. In fact, their hostility was another surprise. Normally people in a strictly regimented situation such as the army readily welcome a basket from home filled with real food. But when Eliab, the eldest, saw David, the youngest, he didn't ask about the folks or the food; he asked only about the sheep—and in a most sarcastic way. "With whom have you left those few sheep in the wilderness?" (verse 28, RSV). The tone is clearly one of condescension and disdain. David's response sounds like a typical reaction of a younger brother who is used to being put down. "What have I done now?" (verse 29, RSV). Eliab's cold treatment of his sibling seems unnecessarily harsh, not entirely unlike an ugly older brother to a male Cinderella. But as the story develops, the reader could conclude that David was not simply a fair-haired precocious little brother, but perhaps a bit pretentious as well. Surely his sense of confidence regarding the Philistine giant would have seemed to the more timid Israelites like overconfidence, and to his older brothers as something akin to egomania.

At the same time, the negative reaction of the elder brother is not that hard to identify with. If a kid brother tagged along with us to work and proceeded to make suggestions to our boss about ways to improve our efficiency, it would take a strong person not to take umbrage at (translate: "throttle") the little brat for his pretentiousness. Actually, such hostile feelings are often aggravated by defensiveness, if the actions of the younger seem to rebuke our timidity or lack of faith. Such was, no doubt, the case here. An army of men, convinced they were fighting not just for territory but also for the honor of the one true God, should not have been cowed by a godless braggart. Young David forced them to confront that very issue—an issue that made them decidedly uncomfortable; hence, the nasty defensiveness.

But when David heard Goliath's bellicose challenges, he couldn't stand such a blasphemous affront to a God he was learning to trust. Of course, his readiness to get involved reveals something about his shepherding experiences. It is easy to pass off David's tending the flock as a means of keeping an otherwise shiftless young person innocently occupied, since it was a harmless and rather meaningless activity. But a shepherd in those days was hardly the equivalent of today's couch potato. Days were long and often alternated between grinding boredom and moments of frantic, breathtaking panic. In addition, there was the constant discomfort of the natural elements. In Genesis 31:39, 40, Jacob describes the rigors of attempting to protect the flock from wild beasts and not always succeeding. He goes on to mention the heat of the day and the frost of the night. It was often a grueling, exhausting job. David clearly didn't have the luxury to sit under a shade tree and compose psalms all day.

To aid his constant challenge of protecting the sheep from various predators, he must have practiced endlessly with the sling. It was not an idle pastime. A good sling was a useful tool of his trade. The velocity such a sling provides for stone throwing is truly awesome—easily life-threatening to marauding man or beast—provided the user has developed a keen accuracy. But accuracy takes an incredible amount of practice and patience. Years ago I made a similar sling and, while in college, I used to go down to the banks of the Saint Joseph River and practice slinging stones at a large tree across the river. The river was quite wide at that point, but I got so I could get a stone in the vicinity of the tree most of the time. I made a similar sling for my roommate, but found it was safer to let him go alone, as he usually managed to spray rocks in totally unexpected directions. After hours of practice I was always glad that I didn't have to hit a target the size of a man—even if he were a giant of a man.

It must have been lonely for David out there in the rocky fields with only nonverbal creatures to talk to. But David didn't succumb to the loneliness or the boredom. He faithfully applied himself to the routine work against that day when he might be confronted by the unexpected. He worked hard at his shepherding, but not simply to prepare for something better in the future. I don't think he wasted much time pining for some golden future job or responsibility that would take him away from these stupid, exasperating sheep. He did his boring homework, found new pastures for the sheep, on occasion tackled and killed a lion and a bear, all as a kind of prelude for the real test that he had no way of anticipating.

It is an important lesson. The daily thistles and thorns are an important preparation for the choking brambles that may come later. The grinding routine of school, the frustrations of work in the marketplace, the seeming limited vision of bosses or coworkers, the agonizing short-sightedness and apparent rebellion of teenage children, the unremitting demands of caring for elderly parents in failing health, all contribute to a wearing down of determination and resolve. Or, if we let them, they can serve as discipline that strengthens and prepares us for even greater tests in the future. It is so tempting to let impatience dominate our thinking, but there are few genuine shortcuts to success that will bypass all the tests that toughen. To change the metaphor, time spent on the daily treadmill of troubles can build endurance for some later massive marathon that will only be successfully completed by a body and spirit made tough by lots of workouts. For David, keeping the sheep was his daily workout. Goliath would be his massive marathon.

And massive he was. His height of six cubits and a span (1 Sam. 17:4) may have been well over nine feet tall. The weight of his armor, at 5,000 shekels, was somewhere in the range of 100 to 220 pounds. The head of his spear, at 600 shekels, was somewhere between 11 and 26 pounds. To say that he was a formidable opponent is a considerable understatement. His challenge to Israel, to send out a worthy opponent so that the two of them could settle the issues of the battle and actually reduce the wider bloodshed (verse 9), was probably a ruse that the Philistines had no intention of honoring. But it was a moot point, as Israel had no one interested in or capable of rising to the challenge. That is, until the little shepherd boy stepped forward.

When David heard the giant's challenge, he quickly realized that here was the human counterpart of those lions and bears that he had already vanquished. But actually accepting the challenge wasn't as easy as David thought it would be. First, it was when he began asking questions about this Philistine that David's brother Eliab tried to intimidate him and get him to head back home to his sheep. When David persisted in his inquiry, he was directed to King Saul, who felt that his youth and inexperience would surely doom him. But David was convinced that his previous hardships with lions and bears had all been part of God's plan to give him the courage to rise to this challenge. Whereupon Saul gave him not only his blessing but also his armor. It was a bad fit—as it always is. God's plan is one suit of armor per person, and it's always custom-tailored. No matter how unhappy we may be with it, and no matter how much we might want someone else's, we can live and work effectively only in our own. Oh, we are free—in fact, obligated—to make adjustments and improvements in our armor/talents, (e.g., David's endless honing of his slinging ability), but we can never successfully adopt someone else's. This is a terrific testimony about God's personal concern. He values each of us for who we are—not for how close we can come to being like saint so-and-so. If we trust in Him, He will make us successful in just the armor with which He has equipped us. But there will be times when that fact will stretch our faith. It must have stretched David's faith a bit, or he would never have bothered to try Saul's armor. But he quickly realized that his limp little sling and God were all the armor he needed. Well, and a few stones. His words sounded very confident ("The Lord . . . will deliver me from the hand of this Philistine" [verse 37, RSV]), but it endears him to my human nature that he picked up five stones and not just one.

As the giant sized up his tiny opponent he was completely flummoxed. He could conclude only two things—either this was a joke, or it was intended to humiliate him. He chose to believe the latter. " 'Am I a dog, that you come to me with sticks?' And the Philistine cursed David by his gods" (verse 43, RSV). Whereupon the giant steps forward to make short work of this little noncontestant. But before the giant can strike a blow, David spells out the nature of the confrontation. The odds don't look that good for little David, but he is not intimidated. In David's mind the giant's weapons are no match for his own: "You come to me with a sword and with a spear and with a javelin; but I come to you in the name of the Lord of hosts, the God of the armies of Israel, whom you have defied" (verse 45, RSV). In fact, David makes quite a verbal assault, before the physical one, by which he promises Goliath that he is about to be defeated. At the same time, in spite of all the time spent practicing with the sling David is absolutely clear about the reason for his victory to come: it will not be because of his prowess. Rather, it will happen "that all the earth may know . . . and that all this assembly may know that the Lord saves not with sword and spear; for the battle is the Lord's and he will give you into our hand" (1 Sam. 17:46, 47, RSV). While it is true that David's first rock found its mark, God was the conquering hero of the day, and David acknowledged as much even before the fact.

This raises an interesting question about the many hours David had spent perfecting his accuracy with the sling. If the battle with Goliath was the Lord's from the very start, David might just as well have been handed his first sling on the way out to meet Goliath. God would see to it that the rock hit Goliath's forehead even if it slipped accidentally from a beginner's sling. But God just doesn't seem to work that way. To say that "the battle is the Lord's" is not to say that all human effort is thereby inconsequential. Such an interpretation could lead a Christian to never get up from his/her knees and go to work. Or it could lead a preacher to do all his/her sermon preparation while driving to the church Sabbath morning. There is clearly an interface between human effort and divine power that will never yield up all its mystery. In other words, we will never fully understand how and why God uses flawed human beings to accomplish many of His ends, when He could much more efficiently use angels. Of course, we have often come to realize that His use of us as His instruments has strengthened and matured us on the way to accomplishing His ends—and that may be as close as we can come to a reason for His using us at all. God might just as well have had Goliath drop dead of a heart attack, or had an angel cast a paralyzing spell over him, as to have David go to the trouble of confronting him. Lessons of faith and human reliance on God's intervention would not have been driven home as powerfully as they were but for that indelible picture: the shepherd boy and his God against the giant and his spear. To the one in a boat on a stormy lake there is an old saying: "Trust in God, but pull for shore." Even though it must often limit Him, God has designed His power to be linked with human effort. "Only a boy named David, only a little sling. Only a boy named David, but he could pray." It wasn't only the sling and it wasn't only the prayer. David's hours and days of practice gave him the assurance so that when the crucial moment arrived, he realized that his hard work had all been part of God's doing. As a result, the larger prayer for the deliverance of Israel could be answered, in part, through his sling. An unanticipated result of his great victory over Goliath was that it served as the catalyst that would transform David from shepherd boy to fugitive. For several years he would be a fugitive from Saul. In time he would become a fugitive from God.

David's victory over the giant, and the resultant rout of the Philistines, catapulted David to hero status and plunged King Saul to next-best. "Saul has slain his thousands, and David his ten thousands" (1 Sam. 18:7, RSV), the people chanted. In addition, the record states, "David had success in all his undertakings; for the Lord was with him" (verse 14, RSV). It was more than the paranoid king could stomach. Whereupon he began a series of deadly plots to eliminate the man he rightly assumed would one day take his place. But every plan was doomed from the outset, because "the Lord . . . had departed from Saul" (verse 12, RSV). As we strive to serve Him, He does not promise us unblemished success in every endeavor. But He does promise that if we rule Him out, we can be assured of ultimate defeat. Saul had decided to take that road, and in time his life would end in an ignominious suicide.

Ironically, David's many successes may have contributed to his inexorable slide off the path of surrender to God into the brambles of self-serving and disobedience. Shouts of acclamation and lots of favorable publicity by the media, and the most single-minded follower of God can fall prey to the powerful desire to believe what the people are saying. The killing of Goliath and the resultant adulation by the crowds must have produced an incredible high for the young shepherd. No doubt he wanted to preserve that moment in the sun as long as possible. How else can we explain David's trudging some 20 miles to Jerusalem carrying as his trophy the bloody, super-large head of the decapitated Goliath (1 Sam. 17:57)? But his euphoria was short-lived—Saul's jealousy flamed to the surface, and David had to run for his life, again and again, for months. In fact, chapter after chapter (1 Sam. 18-26) records little more than an extended series of attempts by Saul to hunt down and kill David. He tried everything, from heaving his own spear at David while he sang (on at least three separate occasions [1 Sam. 18:11; 19:10]), to bribing others to kill him (1 Sam. 19:1), to leading an army of 3,000 to kill him (1 Sam. 24:2). Every attempt failed, often in ways that humiliated Saul. At length, Saul dies ignominiously by his own hand. His suicide was prompted by his fear that if his enemies were to find him wounded, they would not only kill him but would then go on to make sport of him by displaying his corpse. But dying by his own sword failed to spare him that humiliation. The Philistines found his body on the battlefield and made a mockery of him, just as he had feared. It was a pathetic conclusion to a failed royal reign. But now the way is cleared for the previously anointed David to assume his rule.

As he took the royal reins of power, David's popularity seemed to have no limit. During a variety of military campaigns David basked in the acclaim of the people. "It pleased them; as everything that the king did pleased all the people" (2 Sam. 3:36, RSV). But more important, David was well aware of the source of his success. "And David became greater and greater, for the Lord, the God of hosts, was with him" (2 Sam. 5:10, RSV). The text implies that if he were to maintain that close connection with God, he would go on from success to success. At this point in his life he repeatedly sought divine direction before embarking on any military campaign, and the result was that "the Lord gave victory to David wherever he went" (2 Sam. 8:14, RSV). But at this stage of his life and rule, wherever he went there was a battle to be fought, an army to be crushed, enemies that needed killing. "After this David defeated the Philistines. . . . And he defeated Moab. . . . David slew twenty-two thousand men of the Syrians. . . . He slew eighteen thousand Edomites . . . David slew of the Syrians . . . forty thousand horsemen, and wounded Shobach . . . so that he died there" (verses 1-13, RSV; 2 Sam. 10:18, RSV). Whatever else he was, David was clearly a man of extraordinary military prowess.

In the midst of all these successful battles, the prophet Nathan comes to David to speak for God and promises David, "I will make for you a great name, like the name of the great ones of the earth" (2 Sam. 7:9). As if his unblemished military record and frequent human accolades weren't enough, God adds the unequivocal promise of fame. It would be fulfilled beyond his wildest imaginings. He could never know that generations later, huge crowds would link his name to the Messiah as a show of unparalleled adulation.

At the same time, we must guard against the common thought: God grants special privileges and powers to those who perform better in life, to those who accumulate a longer list of good deeds than someone else. His promise to make David's name great was born out of God's ever-present grace, not David's impeccable character. Like all other humans, David took turns running ahead of and away from God. While each transgression is not called such, nor receives a particular reprimand, the details of his life reflect frequent forays into fields filled with the devil's weeds. There he would surely have gotten lost, except for the persistence of Heaven's Hound. For example, 2 Samuel 3 mentions that he had six sons, and it names them—together with the six different women of whom they were born. And all that was after his first marriage to Michal, the daughter of Saul, and prior to the spectacle concerning Uriah and Bathsheba. That immoral minefield should have destroyed him. Today, in spite of a flawed judicial system, a man in our society convicted of taking another man's wife and then murdering her husband would likely spend the rest of his years in prison; and, if paroled, would hardly be reinstated to his former office.

The fact that we know all the dirty little details of the Bathsheba story shows the honesty of the biblical account. It enhances the credibility of a story when its heroes are not presented only in glossy colors. To this point in the story, David comes across as a man for whom everything he touches turns to gold. Every enemy he faces gets defeated. But the enemy from within posed a very different threat. And the flaw was all his own—no outside circumstance could be blamed, for "each person is tempted when he is lured and enticed by his own desire" (James 1:14, RSV). No excuse could be offered. "But she shouldn't have been bathing there!" "But she was so beautiful." The human drive to lessen guilt by casting blame elsewhere dates from the very beginning. "The woman whom thou gavest to be with me, she gave of the tree" (Gen. 3:12). The deflecting finger-pointing began with Adam, but the tendency seems to have picked up steam with the passage of time. Today we put forth incredible effort to squeeze ourselves into the role of victim—a victim who can usually be assuaged by money. We have learned to play the blame game with excruciating finesse.

David's premeditated plotting and careful planning, however, made it impossible for him to play that game later. "He saw from the roof a woman bathing; and the woman was very beautiful. And David sent and inquired about the woman. . . . So David sent messengers, and took her" (2 Sam. 11:2-4, RSV). When he saw her, he was tantalized by her beauty, and he obviously lingered on those thoughts. The thoughts he couldn't help, and they were not sin. It was the lingering that he could help. A healthy, heterosexual male, even a happily married one, suddenly confronted by a partially nude beautiful woman, will find it erotic. In His sermon on the mount Jesus makes reference to something that sounds quite similar, but He acknowledged an important difference. In Matthew 5:28 He said that "every one who looks at a woman lustfully has already committed adultery with her in his heart" (RSV). However, the Greek construction makes it very clear that He was not referring to the involuntary waking of the sex impulse. If that was what He meant, we, like certain Pharisees of old, would have to wear blinders to shield us from the lurid advertising that constantly assaults our eyes. A very literal translation of Matthew's phrases could read, "Everyone who continually looks at a woman with the intent to desire (or for the purpose of desiring) her . . ." Obviously Jesus is referring to the harboring of the thought. A kind of delicious imagining and desiring. No, David's thoughts were not the sin; it was the lingering that lured and enticed him.

Then the harbored thought produced action—he "sent and inquired about the woman" (2 Sam. 11:3, RSV) and learned that she was married. Of course, so was he. At this point he was already well off God's path, but Heaven's Hound tarried. The plot must be allowed to thicken so that human choices and the consequences of those choices can stand out in bold relief. The sin of adultery quickly got more complicated when Bathsheba became pregnant. Unfortunately, David put his position and pride before principle and devised a strategy that he hoped would cover the sin and allow him to appear guiltless. He would recall husband Uriah from the battlefield, send him home to be with Bathsheba, following which her pregnancy would raise no eyebrows. But another complication ensued when high-minded Uriah refused to avail himself of the opportunity of a pleasant night with his wife while his compatriots were struggling on the battlefield. Perhaps, too, he was remembering that when David and his men were committed to a military campaign, they were, during that time, committed to sexual abstinence (1 Sam. 21:4, 5). In any case he chose to sleep outside the king's door with the servants. But David couldn't bring himself to give up the attempt to paper over his sin. So the next evening he literally wined and dined Uriah, getting him drunk and hoping that while Uriah was under the influence his inhibitions would weaken sufficiently for him to go home to his wife. But again David's ploy failed; whereupon he resorted to the ultimate solution—murder. "Sin is like quicksand; the more energetic the human effort to extricate oneself, the deeper the involvement" (Ganse Little, in *The Interpreter's Bible* [Nashville: Abingdon Press, 1953], Vol. II, p. 1098). David brazenly signed Uriah's death warrant and then had the temerity to send it by Uriah's own hand to Joab, instructing him to put Uriah into the heat of battle and then pull back and leave him defenseless. It worked. Uriah was killed, the widow mourned, the widow was brought to the king's house for comfort, David sighed with relief. The subterfuge succeeded. His sin was papered over, and no one was the wiser. No one, that is, except Bathsheba and Joab and, of course, God. Earlier David had been a fugitive on the run from Saul. Now he was a fugitive on the run from God and from his own conscience.

But the wonder of grace is not quenched. In spite of the fact that David had "utterly scorned the Lord" (2 Sam. 12:14, RSV), Heaven's Hound is released to track down the fugitive king and show him the way back. What a message about divine patience, forbearance, forgiveness! David had forged ahead, repeatedly ignoring God's warning voice of restraint and reproof. All along he knew what he was doing, and he knew it was wrong. Still, he moved unflinchingly from one sinful scheme to the next in a desperate attempt to cover his wrongdoing. And just when he thought he was home free, his reverie was interrupted by the noisy baying of Heaven's Hound, except it came subtly embodied in the form of Nathan, the prophet.

Nathan's approach was a masterpiece of storytelling and psychological entrapment. The fictional story of a poor man whose lone little lamb was seized and slaughtered for a rich man's feast is gripping in its simplicity (2 Sam. 12:2-7). The sheer meanness of the rich man's seizure of the poor man's lamb is so transparently wrong that only a person with the conscience of a fence post could fail to condemn it. In fact, David got so caught up with his vigorous condemnation of the unscrupulous man that the application of the story sailed right past him—until, of course, Nathan stabbed him with the stark accusation "Thou art the man!" It shredded the paper with which David had covered his conscience, and he fell to his knees, exposed and condemned. In Psalm 51 he poured out his anguished and pathetic cry of remorse and repentance. The Hound of Heaven had done His work once more.

Admittedly it is easy to say "I'm sorry" when our sin stands completely exposed so that further cover-up would be not only pointless but laughable. But the sentiments David expressed in Psalm 51 carry not a hint of excuse or defensiveness. Instead he repeatedly admits his sin, which is "ever before me" (verse 3), and asks that God might create in him a "clean heart" and put a "new and right spirit within me" (verse 10, RSV). In addition, he moves well beyond the cultural understanding of the day when he acknowledges, "Against thee . . . have I sinned, and done that which is evil in thy sight" (verse 4, RSV). In his time a wife was considered part of the husband's belongings, somewhat similar to, though slightly higher than, his cattle and sheep. So to take another man's wife was widely believed to be a terrible wrong done to the husband, like grand theft, but little more. However, David admits that his sin was not just against Uriah, but was clearly against God. That might strike some as sounding a bit too theological for the modern mind, but it is a weighty point that is often forgotten in the heat of today's psychoanalytic discussions about wrong behavior and guilt. If we reflected more on the impact our sins have on God and our relationship with Him, it would serve as a much greater deterrent than does our rather cavalier attitude toward what we euphemistically call "human mistakes." It was the thought that his behavior had wounded the heart of God that so broke David's.

David clearly understood that the repentance and restitution God expects of His wandering children need not include some expensive sacrifice. "Were I to give a burnt offering, thou wouldst not be pleased. The sacrifice acceptable to God is a broken spirit; a broken and contrite heart, O God, thou wilt not despise . . . then wilt thou delight in right sacrifices" (Ps. 51:16-19, RSV). When we ponder the enormity of David's sins/crimes that God was willing to forgive, the meaning of grace takes on an added luster. Given the immorality, the arranged murder, and the various deceitful cover-ups, we can only stand in awe of the God of such forgiveness.

But the healing balm of forgiveness cannot erase the scars. In spite of his tears of remorse and his anguished prayers and fasting, the son born of adultery lived only a week. During those seven days, the great warrior for God, the "man after [God's] own heart" (1 Sam. 13:14, RSV), fasted and prayed in vain for the life of his baby. The God who had been so close and so directive at so many points in his life retreated into silence while David agonized. Forgiveness and acceptance with God is not a guarantee of deliverance from all the wider consequences of sin. And for years the resulting ripples would continue to spread.

One son, Amnon, would lust after and rape his half sister (2 Sam. 13:14). Another son, Absalom, would murder Amnon and later attempt to seize the throne and murder David. And though David didn't live to see it, his brilliant son Solomon descended into a hedonistic immorality worse than his father's, and took hundreds of wives and concubines who "turned away his heart," so that he "did what was evil in the sight of the Lord" (1 Kings 11:3, 6, RSV). David's waywardness, while forgiven by God, greatly weakened his ability to correct and guide his straying sons. God tracked him down, called him back, forgave him, and gave him a new heart. But then David lived to witness the outworking of the inexorable principle that what we sow we will indeed reap. During his fugitive years David sowed the wind. As a repentant and forgiven sinner, he reaped the whirlwind. He is at once a powerful example and a powerful warning—a powerful example of the long reach of grace and a powerful warning of its limits; a sweeping testimony to forgiveness and reconciliation, and an ominous reminder of the logevity of consequences and scars.

CHAPTER 8

ABSALOM, AMNON, AND TAMAR:
The Price of Pride

SOME BOYS PLAY PRANKS AND ARE RASCALLY, but they grow up and grow out of it and become teachers and administrators. There are some who show little interest in growing up if it means settling down and becoming productive, contributing members of society. For them, age only spurs on the rascally part until it takes on a more sinister coloration so that what once seemed clever and mildly entertaining becomes serious and scary. They keep the Hound of Heaven busy.

Absalom, the son of King David and his wife Maacah, must have had a rascally stage, but by the time we get a good look at him, there's not much left that is clever or entertaining. From the vantage point of the Bible writer, Absalom the man is egotistical, mean-spirited, and rotten to the core. Although if confronted with his punky center, he might have picked up a modern theme and cried, "But it's not my fault—it got rubbed onto me by all the rotten examples around me." And if he had said that, he would have had a point, though not an alibi.

Before further indictment of such royal stock, let's peek into this family and examine some of those influences that must have helped turn a prankster into a killer. Sure enough, the father was hardly a tower of strength before his growing brood. While he had outstanding leadership qualities and was peerless in military organization, he had a lecherous side that would prevent his ever being voted father of the year. The incident with Bathsheba, so well documented by pen and film, was only a small part of a very untidy family unit. For example, while living in

Hebron, David had six sons, all with different mothers. In fact, to number and name and keep track of all David's wives and children would be a challenging assignment. As far as we can tell, his family was large before his moral disaster with Bathsheba and Uriah. If he had an uncontrolled weakness for bathing beauties, could his sons be far behind?

Apparently not. In fact, one son upped the ante on his father's sexual fantasy and zeroed in on his half sister. Tamar was quite beautiful (2 Sam. 13:1), but she was still Amnon's sister. Now, normally the girls or boys you share a bathroom with while growing up become like a worn-out sneaker, so familiar and so boring that the enticing features lose their luster. Not that siblings are valueless. They are, after all, your brother or sister; so you inevitably share a few family traits. But one thing is clear: no one has to warn you not to marry that person who always managed to avoid helping you with the dishes. Some antipathy here is normal, but obviously Amnon wasn't.

Fortunately, his perverse desire for his half sister was hampered by a certain slow-wittedness. His passion told him what he wanted, but his mind gave out under the weight of every plan he could come up with. All he succeeded in doing was making himself sick (verse 2). Enter cousin Jonadab. Amnon was now aided by a voyeur who didn't have to experience everything, so long as he could imagine others going off into the forbidden zone. So when the cousins pooled their brainpower, Jonadab came up with a plan. The fact that it was immoral never even came into their discussion. The complexity of the plan indicates that, while Jonadab was a little quicker than Amnon, they both may have sat in the intellectually challenged part of the classroom. A faked illness is just not a difficult act to script.

At the same time, the family had certain rules. Half brothers and sisters were to avoid suggestive relationships unless they have the king's permission. As it turned out, it was not all that hard to obtain. A slight bending of the truth about how Tamar's biscuits would rejuvenate him if she baked them in his presence (verse 8), and his wish became the king's command. His malingering worked, and Tamar brought her pots and pans right into the "sick room." Amnon was truly sick, but not in the way Tamar was led to believe. Actually, she can be excused for falling into his trap, because his intentions were too foul to have crossed her mind. She was apparently familiar with his undeveloped power of reasoning as she tried to slow him down with some very simple but questionable reasoning of her own. "Just be up front with your father—tell him you want me, and he will probably give his approval." Yeah, right! Amnon is no quick study, but even he knows David's morals won't bend that far.

Her appeal to Amnon's clouded mind failed, and he forced himself upon her. The result was not at all what he had expected. Forbidden pleasures may seem the sweetest, but only until they are experienced. The excitement is in the chase. We humans can't seem to learn the lesson of the dogs that chase cars. When the dog catches the car, the excitement is all over and the bewildered animal isn't quite sure what to do. But with humans it is much more serious than that. If seizing the forbidden fruit brings guilt, we often skip right over the satisfaction stage to disappointment and disgust. "Then Amnon hated her with very great hatred; so that the hatred with which he hated her was greater than the love with which he had loved her" (verse 15, RSV). The pleasures that last and continue to reward us are those that follow control, restraint, and even discipline.

When Absalom learns of his half brother's moral collapse, he is livid but controlled. The best face we can put on his seething anger is that he wanted justice to be done and waited for his father to do it. But as time stretched on, his anger turned into hatred. His moral outrage over his violated half sister was not wrong. An indictment of our time is that so little stirs us to cry out against outrageous behavior. Our sensitivities have been so cauterized by the shocks of depravity that in the place of nerve endings we have only scar tissue. A consuming zeal for right and justice causes an occasional ripple in the news; but then, tolerant apathy once again rules. But Absalom was neither tolerant nor apathetic. His sense of justice, however, was tinged with a smoldering hatred that he would nurse in secrecy for two whole years.

The sad fact is that King David, the father of the clan, turned his back on his responsibility to redress the wrong. He was the father of the benighted Amnon and the leader of a people. His responsibility to provide moral direction and justice was doubly important. Yet he continued to ignore the incident and what he should do about it. Of course, his own recent moral lapse with Bathsheba continued to cause embarrassment, and terribly weakened his ability to lead. How could he take control and show moral courage in dealing with his wayward son when his own example was still shouting failure? It is wonderful to depend upon the Hound of Heaven to find us and lead us back, but shortsightedness often lets us forget that we accumulate scars that people won't let us forget. And like it or not, when we assume a mantle of leadership, we assume, for most observers, a higher standard of behavior. David knew his people's high expectations and he knew his failure, so he hoped that for a while he wouldn't have to mediate problems of moral behavior in others. He needed some time to demonstrate penance and show that his moral center was not completely hollow. That he had followed Heaven's Hound back to the path of faith. But the evil one was determined to give him no such time for character rebuilding. David's musings probably went something like: "Of course, Amnon was an immoral man; we all have our failures, so let's not be too judgmental." Maybe David even sensed that someday there would be such a saying as "He that is without sin among you, let him first cast a stone." No, it would be better just to forget this sorry chapter in the family and move on with our lives. Let's not take any action just yet.

But there is a difference between passing pretentious judgment on a fellow traveler, who in most respects is our moral equal, and allowing awful injury and injustice to go unchallenged. If David were to take some action against Amnon, he would not be judging him—God's law had done that already. Still, executing the sentence was left with the king to carry out; but delay became the order of the day. Justice endlessly delayed is simply another form of injustice.

Furthermore, this injustice was aggravated because it all happened with such high-profile people. It just wasn't the kind of story that would be whispered around a few royal hallways but kept from the masses. While the people of Israel didn't have our racy telecommunications, their process of rumoring must have been quite efficient. Amnon's lechery was soon public knowledge. I can just hear Absalom muttering to himself, "How blind and deaf can a person be? Is my father the only person in this nation who isn't aware of all the grumbling about the lax morals in the royal palace? Everybody knows. It's an embarrassment. The royal family needs some serious cleaning up, and if necessary, I am not only willing but eager to do it."

By now Absalom had strayed far from the path of justice and faith and was thoroughly lost among the brambles of his resentment and anger. Too much time had elapsed; months had turned into two years, and still David, the rightful authority, had done nothing to redress Amnon's wrong. Every rape is horrible, but the account of this one underscores that fact by informing us that Tamar is not only the sister of the perpetrator, but also beautiful and a virgin (verses 1, 2). Surely her violation could not go unpunished. Absalom loved his sister and would later name his own daughter after her (2 Sam. 14:27), but he was not the man to bring justice to Amnon, and his method was probably not what God had in mind. How the Hound of Heaven counseled him we can never know, but the passage of two years strongly suggests that Absalom was experiencing conflict about his course of action. Surely the divine presence had caught up with Absalom and was suggesting patience and a better way.

But finally Absalom turned away from that insistent voice and decided to find his own way out of the wilderness of rage. It was a tragic mistake. Since he was the intellectual superior of his half brother, he had no difficulty coming up with a plan, which he deviously put into action. The murder took place at the sheepshearing, which is always a bustling, frenetic activity for sheep farmers. First Absalom's servants got Amnon drunk (2 Sam. 13:28), then they killed him—all at Absalom's bidding. But to cover his tracks, Absalom had earlier invited the king to accompany him to the sheepshearing, strongly (and correctly) suspecting that he would turn down the invitation, but also figuring that the invitation would mask any complicity on Absalom's part. "Absalom couldn't possibly have done such a thing. Why, he even invited the king to go along with him to the sheepshearing. Why would he invite the king if he were planning to murder his half brother? No, surely someone else is responsible." But even though many in Israel would rush to support the handsome prince and hotly deny his involvement, Absalom felt the part of wisdom was a self-imposed exile until things had a chance to calm down a bit. So he fled to Geshur and tried for a while to keep a low profile.

So now flagrant immorality and murder have besmirched the royal siblings, but all is quiet among the legal counselors. Shouldn't something be done about it? There are times when it's best to let "sleeping dogs lie"; arousing them creates only commotion and noise, and nothing good comes of it. But if the dog should die, you can't just keep stepping over it, pretending nothing is really there. Someone has to go to the trouble of removing it, or conditions are going to get much worse. In the case of Absalom, it wasn't a body that was beginning to decompose; it was the morality of the royal family. Ignoring it will only spread the infection. But just as David had no stomach for confronting Amnon's immorality, he was just as frightened to do anything about his murder. Since he had strayed so far from the path of morality, it was now harder for him to lead others through the briars to safety. But what kind of statement was his inaction making? Must the nation's leaders now wink at every crime? Must the crimes be worse than rape and murder to require punishment?

So David the king rules in Jerusalem; and Absalom, the self-confessed murderer and handsome prince, lives a few miles away in Geshur, and everybody knows they aren't talking. Three years of this stalemate is more than Joab can take. Joab, David's general and chief military adviser, has known him for years and feels terrible about the rupture in the royal family. In addition to eating away at David's effectiveness as king, it is killing soldier morale. The military people want to feel that behind a stable government stands a stable royal family. But with the prince living in exile under a cloud of murder, there is only scary speculation about what the future of this government might be. So Joab, not blessed with an abundance of patience in the best of circumstances, grabs the reins, and immediately the horse begins to gallop. He finds a "wise woman" (2 Sam. 14:2), in effect, an actress, writes for her a true-to-life but fictional script, and the action begins.

In the first scene the actress plays a widow woman with two very scrappy sons. It is Cain and Abel revisited. One kills the other; and the family, who are not of the pro-life persuasion, wants blood vengeance. Accordingly, the hotheaded brother must pay with his life. The application of this fiction is quite transparent, but the actress is so talented that David doesn't make the connection. Instead he tries to put her off with that most common parental stall for nagging children, "We'll see." He does seem to promise action, but the terms are so general and so perfunctory that she is not convinced that anything much will happen. "Go on home," he tells her, "and I will come up with some orders to resolve your problem." Not good enough. That answer is just a step above "I'll appoint a committee to look into it."

But there are two or three more scenes to follow. Instead of saying, "Fine, thanks, King; I knew I could count on you," and bowing out the door, she holds him a bit longer by volunteering to take any resulting blame. "Now, King, if your action on behalf of my killer son causes any repercussions, be sure to tell people that I am to blame, not you. I would hate for your reputation to be tarnished on my account." She seems to be suggesting that quite a few people are involved and that things could get a little messy. But David, so timid when dealing with his own wayward children, can get quite bellicose when dealing with faceless culprits. "Don't worry; I'll handle all the repercussions. If anyone tries to intimidate you in any way, he'll only try it once (see verse 10).

Surely now she has gotten his commitment to action, so she is content to leave it at that. Not quite. She wants to tie him up so tight that there is no possibility of his wriggling free. "Let the king invoke the Lord your God, that there be no blood vengeance, so that the boy can be assured of life." She knows how important the divine oath is for the rulers of her day. Whenever they uttered those solemn words *"As the Lord lives"* or the equivalent of "as God is my witness," that was a pledge no human would dare to break. So when the actress finally gets David to say, "As the Lord lives, not one hair of your son shall fall to the ground" (verse 11, RSV), she knows she has him right where she wants him. He is now in a corner, where the only way out is the way of compliance.

Since David still seems a bit dense in making the connection, the actress decides she needs to make it for him. She may be a bit fearful for her own safety, but she is now so sure her ruse has worked, so sure that the king will have to keep his word and save Absalom, that he wouldn't dare to kill the one who helped him resolve the Absalom problem. Taking her courage in hand she says, in effect, "King, let's do an instant replay of what just happened here, and see if you can catch my point. You had two sons who quarreled, and one killed the other one. Now some of the people want vengeance on the exiled killer—are you beginning to see a connection to my story and to your promise?" But she can't quite bring herself to come clean on all the details, so she makes one last stab at the fiction, by referring to herself and her son as still needing the king's intercession (verse 16). Then with a flourish of flattery, "My lord the king is like the angel of God to discern good and evil" (verse 17, RSV), she heads for the door.

But now David has suddenly put some things together and smells conspiracy. "Just a moment, young woman. Before you leave, you need to clarify something: Did Joab put you up to this?" She was a good actress, but the whole point of her act was to get David to change his behavior. Still, she must have worried just a bit at what David might do when he discovered that her hotheaded-sons story was fiction. She has done her job well and now just wants to get out, so after admitting that she was Joab's mouthpiece, she resorts once more to some rather sweeping flattery about David's incredible angelic wisdom "to know all things that are on the earth" (verse 20, RSV), and it works. He lets her go.

So Joab, with some female help, has caused David to see that there are people who prefer poor justice to stalemate. Furthermore, Absalom had a following. Clearly he had a way with people that Amnon probably never had. It is not that they approved of ignoring Amnon's murder, but in the human scheme of things time heals wounds and also dulls the sharp edge of moral perception. Absalom is a handsome prince, and if he is not going to be punished for his crime, then let's get the kingdom back on track with a duly recognized prince in line for the throne.

David gets that message, but takes a strange half step. Absalom and many of the people want reconciliation and closure of the early sad chapters. David's moral perception simply won't allow it. Absalom can return to Jerusalem, but he must not live in the royal palace. *I must continue to show my disapproval of his act so there will be no personal reconciliation. One who murders a sibling and expresses no remorse cannot be given indication that he has royal approval. He can live in his own apartment, but I refuse to speak to him or have any dealings with him.* It is a sad story of headstrong youth and parental weakness.

And what a "youth" it was. Absalom's physical presence was totally captivating to all who came into contact with him. According to 2 Samuel 14:25-27 Absalom's appearance and overall bearing must have been enough to cause the average person to catch his/her breath. There wasn't even a good comparison in all of Israel. Pick your current heartthrob, add 10 or so percentage points (or however you tally physical handsomeness), and you might have an Absalom equivalent. "From the sole of his foot to the crown of his head there was no blemish in him" (verse 25, RSV). Unfortunately, it captivated Absalom as well as those around him. Few men attempt to make haircuts a part of their permanent record. Such an event is just not that memorable—unless you are

Absalom. He was fascinated by his own hair. How else can you explain the reference in this greatest of history books to a man's annual haircut, which concluded with the ritual of sweeping up and weighing the hair and recording the amount—a very hefty five pounds! (verse 26). Clearly Absalom's mirror was very kind to him.

As the story unfolds, there is another important lesson tucked away in all Absalom's breathtaking talent and good looks. While youth and beauty need not be faulted, they should not be lionized. We fawn over those who grace the magazine covers. We envy their flawless skin and perfect features. Of course, we occasionally give lip service to the mature idea that inner qualities outrank skin-deep beauty, but all the while we would love to experience the exhilaration of those drop-dead good looks. But the experience of Absalom should grab us by the throat and yell, "Beauty by itself is not a godsend!" Unchecked, our fascination with physical attractiveness can be the most powerful drug of all. A few extra drops on the seed of human nature, and the weed of pride can spring up with alarming speed and disastrous results. Often our hearts and prayers go out for the sad-faced, ungifted ugly ducklings in our midst. Because of their below-average status in life, they seem to be in need of above-average amounts of divine help and intervention. But the story of Absalom brings up an interesting counterpoint. Those who are heavily gifted, who have all the looks and talents, are, in their own way, children at risk. They often stand in special need of the prayers and intercession of caring loved ones and believers. We are prone to feel that with all their natural good looks and good fortune, they are more likely to make it on their own. But Absalom raises an important caution to any such conclusion.

While Absalom is now back in the capital city, his past is forgiven but hardly forgotten. He and his father are not yet reconciled. David has bowed to public pressure and allowed Absalom to return, but has refused to see him. David knows he should have taken more decisive action, but by keeping him at arm's length, he can continue to indicate his disapproval of Absalom's actions. It is weak, it is a stalemate, but it is something. The amazing thing is that David is able to keep the arrangement in place for two whole years.

It has now been five years since the murder and seven years since the event that got it all started. Obviously, time doesn't heal all wounds. Some fester and turn deadly. In Absalom's case, an infection was growing that was about to erupt in a frightening form. The strained relationship with his father hamstrung the princely perks, and all the people knew it. It was downright galling. Since no sentence had been pronounced, Absalom figured that five years of probation was enough. He sent for Joab, who had choreographed his return from Geshur to Jerusalem. But Joab wanted no further involvement. He had gotten father and son back into the same town; it was up to them to work out the barrier between them. Joab sent Absalom his regrets. But after two invitations and two refusals Absalom takes action that can't be denied—he torches Joab's barley field. Absalom's need to get his own way has become pathological. "Then Joab arose and went to Absalom at his house." I guess so! But when he asks Absalom to explain his violent action, Absalom's response is the callous retort "I sent for you and you didn't come!" In his mind a crop of barley is nothing compared to the wish of the prince. His thicket of self-importance is closing in around him.

A final gesture of intercession by Joab brings father and son together at last. There is a royal embrace, the tragic chapter of the past is closed, and both king and prince begin the rest of their lives. But for Absalom the final chapter begins right where the previous one closed. Though he had "bowed himself on his face to the ground before the king" (2 Sam. 14:33, RSV), his spirit was unaffected by that lowly posture. In fact, David's kiss of reconciliation became the kiss of power for Absalom. At last he could finally begin acting like the prince he really was. The first thing he needed was a sense of freedom and independence; and, then as now, that meant his own set of wheels. "After this Absalom got himself a chariot and horses, and fifty men to run before him" (2 Sam. 15:1, RSV). Apparently the thrill was in the independence, not the speed, since all those men could run in front of him and not get run over. He was now a happy traveler, although at that speed he would never have bugs on his teeth.

But happy is not necessarily content. This is the problem with pride; it can never be quite content as long as there is anyone just a bit brighter or more powerful or better looking. No one was better looking than Absalom, but as long as David occupied the throne, Absalom would always be less than number one. When pride is given its head, nothing that stands in its way is safe, even when it is one's own father. So Absalom set about to steal the hearts of the people of Israel. And he was successful. By flattery and deceit he convinced hordes of people that, if he were king, he would see to it that their wishes were granted. In the short term, popularity is not that difficult to gain, even for people of average talents. How easy it must have been for the talented, congenial Absalom. The good guys don't always win. Sometimes they come in dead last. And except for some divine intervention, David was about to be both of those. Absalom's plan was both sinister and deadly. Since he could never be content to be assistant king and since they couldn't have two kings over the same kingdom and since David had no reason to step down, Absalom would have to kill his father.

In the last year or so, Absalom had honed his skills at political promise-making, kissing all comers, and various other gestures of opportunistic glad-handing (verses 3-5). Finally his following and power base were large enough to give him the courage and audacity to proclaim himself king at Hebron, a city some distance from Jerusalem. However, in order to take David's throne, he would have to beat him on the field of battle; and that, for Absalom, was a formidable undertaking. As a backslapper he was peerless; as a military strategist he was out of his element. His only hope for success would be if he could obtain some inside information about David's plans and whereabouts.

That very information suddenly appeared in the form of Hushai the Archite, also known as Hushai the turncoat. Except Hushai was a sort of double turncoat, planted by David to give misinformation. Known as a trusted adviser of David, Hushai's sudden appearance in Absalom's camp caused some misgivings at first; but his reassurances of switched loyalties seemed genuine, and Absalom believed him. When Absalom asked his advice on military strategy, he counseled caution and a go-slow policy of attack, since David was enraged like a she-bear robbed of her cubs. In actuality, Absalom's subtle buildup of power, coupled with David's naïveté about his devious son, caused Absalom's sudden coup to come as a colossal surprise to the king. Had Absalom quickly followed his seizure of power with a rapid attack, the surprised and disorganized David might well have been defeated.

That was precisely the way Ahithophel, Absalom's trusted adviser, saw it and advised. He counseled Absalom to go after David at once, while he was still fleeing from Jerusalem and completely disorganized. Of all the advisers of the time, Ahithophel was held in the highest respect by both David and Absalom. But this time other forces were at work to defeat the wisdom of his counsel. While it is true that in the short term good guys don't always win and sometimes actually lose quite badly, it is also true that in the long term the bad guys are going to lose. In the short term Absalom had won many hearts, but he represented pride and all the grief that comes with it. On the other hand, in this immediate conflict David represented selflessness and humility—the logical and theological opposite of Absalom. For example, as David and his closest advisers were fleeing Jerusalem before organizing their battle plan, some of his men came bringing the ark, with the idea that this would ensure God's presence on their side of the battlefield. But David would have none of it. He told them to take it back into the city, and if he found favor in the eyes of the Lord, he would see the ark again. He knew that God's presence and power are not to be seized, but surrendered to. On the other hand, like the devil himself, Absalom was attempting to "ascend above the heights," and seize that which was not his. Such grasping pride could not be allowed to win, but God would have to intervene to keep it from happening. The lesson that pride can end only in defeat had to be made. So for reasons not understood at the time, the counsel of Hushai was taken over the counsel of the impeccable Ahithophel. Absalom would wait a bit and make very certain his plan of attack. As soon as that decision was reached, the insightful Ahithophel knew that Absalom would lose, so he promptly committed suicide rather than go down in defeat with Absalom and his men.

By the time the battle began, the now-well-organized David was ready; and Absalom had no chance. But as the platoon leaders rode off to meet the attack, the final instructions of David must have seemed quite out of sync with the circumstances: "Deal gently for my sake with the young man, even with Absalom" (2 Sam. 18:5). Surely one of them must have responded with something like "But Your Majesty, he is a killer, and you're at the top of his list." But that made no impact on David's father heart. His plan to save the kingdom simply could not include the death of his son.

It was not a lengthy battle, but it was terribly costly—20,000 men. "The battle spread over the face of all the country; and the forest devoured more people that day than the sword" (verse 8, RSV). Pride is always costly. Rarely does it affect just the person involved. Others are quickly caught up in the consequences. The first time it erupted, it dragged off a third of the most intelligent beings in the universe into the wilderness of confusion and death (Rev. 12:4). Here, the pride of one man resulted in the death of thousands.

Absalom soon wished that he had paid closer attention when his father had sat with his sons and described his many military exploits. Things quickly went bad for Absalom and his men, and they were soon in full flight, which is a bit tricky when you are on horseback or muleback and trees with low-hanging branches are thick. Then, in one of the most humiliating indignities imaginable, the handsome and truly dashing prince misjudges a limb and is swept cleanly from the saddle, his head caught firmly in a branch. Some scholars feel that his long and beautiful hair, with which he was so enamored, was a complicating part of his unsuccessful ride through the trees. David's parting counsel to be compassionate with Absalom registered deeply in the minds of all his men, so when one of them found the desperate prince dangling but alive, he could not bring himself to administer the coup de grâce. Joab, however, had no such qualms. He viewed the situation in much more practical terms. The gauntlet Absalom had thrown down made it very clear: this was a fight to the death. If one of the two must die, Joab would do everything in his power to make sure it wasn't David. At this moment Absalom was helpless, but Joab was convinced that David and his kingdom would never be safe as long as Absalom lived. So he killed him and gave him a hasty, unroyal burial (2 Sam. 18:17).

When the news came back that the battle was over and his kingdom was safe, David had only one concern: "Is it well with the young man Absalom?" (verse 32, RSV). The answer crushed him, and he could only sob out his grief, "O my son Absalom, my son, my son Absalom! Would I had died instead of you, O Absalom, my son, my son!" (verse 33, RSV).

The scripture asserts that the battle was lost because the "forest devoured more people . . . than the sword." But it wasn't the forest of Ephraim that destroyed Absalom. He didn't die just because his mule got lost and he rode under the wrong tree. Absalom died because, in spite of warnings, he had repeatedly wandered deep into the thicket of self-importance, the most dangerous of all the brambles. While the Hound of Heaven could still find him, the cost for this kind of rescue is high—like having to say, "I'm sorry," or stopping to ask for directions. You first must admit you are lost; and for pride, that is the hardest test of all.

CHAPTER 9

JONAH:
The Most Famous Flight From God

HOW IRONIC. HIS NAME MEANT "DOVE" and was viewed as a term of endearment. But his story suggests that few people would think warm, "dovey" thoughts at the mention of Jonah's name. He was opinionated, narrow-minded, and headstrong. He would argue a point and disagree with anybody—even God Himself. Once he took a stand, no amount of reasoning or logic would budge him. Sometimes we say, with some admiration, "There's a person of conviction." Other times we say with despair, "Would a fool be more stubborn?" With the benefit of hindsight, we can see that Jonah fits the latter category, though at the time, the distinction would have been more difficult. In any case, Jonah didn't strike any of his townsfolk as all that dovelike. Although, after watching the feisty doves at my bird feeder, I get the feeling that perhaps Jonah's parents were on to something. But we must re-create the setting before his story will make much sense.

It was a time of rampant prosperity in Israel. Evidences of success and luxury were everywhere. From their well-appointed homes to their well-stocked pantries (Amos 6:4), Israelites were living comfortably. In recent times Israel had been the victor in its wars with nearby nations. National boundaries were extended more widely than at any time in recent memory. In such a time, attitudes of contentment and self-satisfaction begin to well up. Sometimes they're even tinged with a bit of smugness. Nothing like concern or compassion for neighbors was cropping up in any Israelite breast. In fact, "an ugly, narrow, selfish nationalism had developed in their hearts" (Kyle Yates, *Preaching From the Prophets* [Nashville: Broadman Press, 1942], p. 187). If a man known as a prophet would go to extreme ends to avoid sharing a saving message with a neighboring city, just how narrow was the nationalism of the man on the street? To understand the depth of that nationalistic spirit is the first step in understanding the real message of the book of Jonah. A spirit of isolationism had seized many in Israel, and the story of Jonah "is designed as a counterblast to that policy" (W. Neil, "Book of Jonah," *The Interpreter's Dictionary of the Bible,* ed. George A. Buttrick [Nashville: Abingdon Press, 1962], vol. 2, p. 964). It would actually come as a shock to many of those Israelite leaders to be told that their understanding of God was not to be viewed as their exclusive property, but was to be shared with the entire Gentile world. In that respect, "the book of Jonah is . . . to be reckoned among those Old Testament writings which come closest to the spirit of the Christian gospel" *(ibid.)*.

So far, each of our fugitives was part of a larger story within which they played a role. In contrast, Jonah's story is complete in itself and comprises an entire book of the Bible, albeit a very small one. And by any measure, it was a most unusual book and story. In fact, among the prophets, Jonah is truly unique. Other prophets hammer away at the foibles of Israel. In contrast, Jonah is directed to leave Israel, has no words for his people, and precious few for the people to whom he is sent. His entire message is summed up in eight words: "Yet forty days, and Nineveh shall be overthrown" (Jonah 3:4). In addition, the focus of the other prophets is outward, highlighting the problems of the people and politics around them. Small attention is usually paid to the person of the prophets—what they thought or where they went or what they did. With Jonah, however, our attention is continually focused on the man himself—his actions, his attitudes, his thoughts, his misadventures. Finally, while other prophets sometimes answered their call with reluctance (Jer. 1:6), Jonah took reluctance to an entirely new level. Moses didn't want the job God offered him either, but in his bargaining dialogue he listened to God's offer and eventually was willing to strike a deal. But Jonah hatched a scheme that he hoped would prevent any possible dialogue. Prophets became known as God's spokesmen. Jonah became known as God's most famous fugitive.

When you think seriously about the details, Jonah's story is so incredible at so many points that it is hardly surprising that many scholars have questioned its historicity. Think about the details. A prophet of God thinks he can escape "the presence of the Lord" (Jonah 1:3). As he flees, a storm threatens the boat, until he is thrown overboard; then immediately all is calm. He is returned to his mission only after being swallowed by a very large fish. His three days and nights in the fish give him time, not to be digested, but to compose a psalm, after which he is spit out on the very beach he had tried to flee and is no worse for the wear from his entombment. He delivers his message with vigor, and is the only evangelist on record who bitterly laments his success when the entire populace repents. A gourd grows so fast that in one day it provides shade for the overheated Jonah. God then sends a worm to eat the vine and thus teach Jonah a lesson. That is quite a litany of miracles. For some people, that many miracles in a row push the limits of credibility.

Though the fantastic elements may push some people's faith to the breaking point, the historicity of the story has considerable support. For example, in addition to the book of Jonah, 2 Kings 14:25 casually refers to Jonah the son of Amittai as the prophet who foretold the great expansion of Israel's borders during the reign of Jeroboam II. It must have been the same Jonah. In addition to that acknowledgment in Israelite history, there is the reference by Jesus, recorded by both Matthew and Luke (Matt. 12:39-41; Luke 11:29, 30), that assumes that Jonah was a real person. In those passages Jesus states that He would be in the tomb the same amount of time that Jonah was in the belly of the fish, and refers to the repentance of the Ninevites as if it were a historical fact. If Jonah's story is not to be read as history, we have to explain Jesus' references to him.

God's selection of Jonah for this role is intriguing. If God knew that Jonah would run, what was the point in extending the invitation? One answer that springs quickly to mind is the patience of the God of grace. But in Jonah the issues are more complicated. God could have directly confronted Israel's narrow nationalism by sending an angel or a prophet to tell them that they needed to share their God with the pagan nations of the world, such as the Assyrians. Instead He invited a bullheaded man, whose initial refusal and subsequent follow-up comprise a story about evangelism that is much more powerful and long remembered than any overt instruction would have been. Also, God set up all the various details of the story so that everything fit together to teach the lesson God wanted to get across. In that respect it has the appearance of a parable, but packs an even more powerful punch than a parable, since it is actual history.

If God's burden was to reprimand Israel's exclusivist attitude, He chose a highly unusual way to get His point across. First of all, He picked an audience for Jonah, made up of the most unlikely people He could find. Probably no people around them were more despised by Israel than the Assyrians. Their cruelty to the people they conquered had become legendary. If Jonah's argument with God had been recorded, it might have gone something like this: "But God, those people have no regard for the value of human life, let alone for the value of spiritual things. Why send me on a mission that will not only not fulfill its goal, but probably get me killed in the process? On the remote possibility that they might repent, look what a mess that would be—You'd have rank pagans putting on some light covering of religion and attempting to mix in among us—the true believers. It just shouldn't happen. I'm sorry, but I simply can't be a part of something so totally wrongheaded." But this story is another example of God's "in your face" style of confronting a narrow, human concept. As we have repeatedly shown, God seems to like to take a seemingly impossible situation and resolve it dramatically—not so He can say "Ha-ha" when it's over, but so we can say "Aha" as it unfolds. In other words, sending Jonah to preach to the Ninevites so as to teach Israel about the universal gospel was not unlike telling an infertile couple that they will be the mother and father of a huge nation of people. Of course, neither of these "difficult" situations poses a problem for God, only for persons of weak-to-mediocre faith—Jonah, for example, or perhaps you or me.

It certainly did start off all wrong. Jonah is invited to go one way, and he promptly sets off in the opposite direction. His purpose is unmistakably clear—to escape from the "presence of the Lord" (Jonah 1:3). The task from which he wanted to be released was not a small one. The Ninevites were considered by Jews to be godless and cruel, and the city was enormous. Jonah had been raised in a village about four miles north of Nazareth and had seen only cities like Samaria (covering some 20 acres) and possibly the great Jerusalem (covering about 85 acres). So when God asked him to go to Nineveh, an "enemy" city covering some 1,700 acres, it is not surprising that Jonah looked for an out—any out. Who would not be intimidated by the assignment? Still, the solution he came up with was more than a little extreme. His hoped-for destination, Tarshish, is thought by many to be Tartessus in southern Spain, near Gibraltar, some 2,200 miles from Joppa, more than three times the distance to Nineveh (*The Seventh-day Adventist Bible Commentary,* vol. 4, p. 994). It was the farthest known distance from Palestine by sea. Jonah was serious about getting away!

But from "the presence of the Lord"? How could a prophet ever conclude that such a venture could succeed? Where on this earth is "away from the presence of the Lord" (NRSV)? A common belief among many ancient people was that the gods were territorial, and that, by travel, you could actually leave the domain of one god and enter that of another. Is it possible that Jonah, even temporarily, subscribed to that narrow concept of God? How different his thoughts must have been from the plaintive cry of the psalmist, "Whither shall I go from thy Spirit? Or whither shall I flee from thy presence? . . . If I take the wings of the morning and dwell in the uttermost parts of the sea, even there thy hand shall lead me, and thy right hand shall hold me" (Ps. 139:7-10, RSV). Did Jonah actually believe that if he could just get to Tarshish he would be out of the reach of the God of Israel? It seems so.

Most believers today speak of Jonah's flight with only derision. But we moderns should tread softly on this ground of criticism until we have analyzed the reasoning behind some of our own escape attempts. We are much more subtle and restrained in our words and actions, but our flights from God, and from spiritual responsibilities, are often as unthinking or irrational as was Jonah's. For example, we not only tend to spurn God's various invitations to service, but do so in the light of, and in spite of, the instruction that comes from such biblical stories as Jonah's. Hence, our flights away from the path of service are no less excusable than Jonah's frantic attempt. In fact, a certain justifiable fear helped drive Jonah from the path of obedience. It is often simple neglect and weak faith that sidetracks us from our mission. But the end result is much the same. His goal for us is in one direction, and we casually but knowingly head in the opposite.

Having made his strange decision, he went "down into the inner part of the ship" (Jonah 1:5, RSV), where he promptly fell asleep. Was he, at that point, a contented man, comfortable with the thought that he had outsmarted his God; that he would soon be beyond His reach? But when the storm broke, the sleeping prophet had a sudden and rude awakening. The captain of the ship was less than amused to find a passenger sleeping in the midst of their life-threatening situation, and sharply rebuked Jonah with the question "What do you mean, you sleeper?" (verse 6, RSV). The Hebrew word for "sleeper" here is the word used for a deep, unconcerned sleep—which seems so inexplicable, given his situation. The captain reflected the common superstition of the ancients, that there were numerous gods with differing areas under their power. Accordingly, he appealed to Jonah to pray to his god, hoping that if Jonah's god was the angry one, a prayer to him might appease his anger so that their lives might be spared.

But what irony is this? A pagan captain appeals to a prophet to pray to his god, which, in this case, just happens to be the God of heaven, from whom the prophet is trying desperately to escape. Did Jonah begin to suspect that his escape was not going to be trouble-free? Was it beginning to register on his stubborn mind that you can run, but you can't hide or successfully escape from God? If Jonah responded to the captain's appeal by turning to God in prayer, there is no indication of it. In fact, it appears that Jonah gave no clue to anyone about his escape plan until a little later, when he had no choice. Only after the sailors cast lots and the lot fell on Jonah did he open up and begin to tell his story. If there is one thing that these stories make crystal clear, it is that heaven's ways of tracking and calling us are more diverse and varied than we can even imagine. To put it another way, the Hound of Heaven makes His appearance in an endless number of disguises. We are quite prone to limit His "faces." At a tender age we are taught that God appeals to us through His Holy Spirit, through His printed word, through angels, through godly parents, and, on rare occasions, through friends. But through a storm? Through the casting of lots by pagans? Through a huge fish? And all this just to get Jonah back to his original mission.

When the sailors' lot-casting pointed to Jonah as the culprit, they plied him with a battery of embarrassing questions. Speaking from their pagan perceptions, their first question was: who was really responsible? It was obvious to them that Jonah was somehow involved, but they figured that because the storm was so sudden and so threatening, it had to be the work of a god. They wanted to know not just the identity of this god of storms, but something about him. After all, they were sailors, and storms were some of their greatest fears. They wanted to know as much as possible about the god of storms. Theirs was a commonly held understanding that the gods were easily offended, capricious in their judgments, but approachable if done carefully and with the right appeasement offering. Parts of that idea are still around. Some contemporary Christians really feel that a larger offering or a faithful tithe or accepting a mission appointment or going into the ministry will make them, somehow, more acceptable to God. We know better than to use the term *appeasement offering,* but the notion of bonus points with God is not a great deal better. But the sailors' question was fraught with urgency: "Tell us, on whose account this has evil come upon us?" (verse 8, RSV). And then more questions came pouring out: "What is your occupation? And whence do you come? What is your country? And of what people are you?" (verse 8, RSV). The superstitious sailors are at once intrigued by this stranger and terrified of his God. I can hear them now: "Isn't this just great. We have with us a runaway whose god just happens to be one of the storm gods who is so mad he is about to kill this guy by sinking our ship. It isn't fair, but that's the way the gods do things, and there's nothing we can do about it except get all the answers we can from this strange fellow." "So, Jonah, tell us more about yourself, your religion, your god. And please hurry; we're getting a bit desperate, since it looks like we don't have much time."

Now, with his entire plan exposed and certain death riding on every enormous wave, Jonah has just been given an opening to share his faith. But what an opening he has created for himself. In faith sharing we often feel that the most difficult part is trying to figure out a good opening. When people ask us to tell them about ourselves and our religious history, we are usually pleased that the "opening" has been taken out of our hands, and we are more than happy to take it from there. It just makes it so much easier when others take the initiative and ask, "So just what do Adventists believe?" But Jonah's big opportunity is a mixed blessing at best, and his abbreviated answer to their questions is not much of a glowing testimony to the Lord. How could it be, given his situation?

Jonah's response has got to be one of the briefest "witnessing statements" on record. "I am a Hebrew; and I fear the Lord, the God of heaven, who made the sea and the dry land" (verse 9, RSV). In their superstition the sailors are now really terrified, because if, as this man has said, this god rules heaven and also the sea and dry land, then it is obvious that this storm that is wreaking havoc with the sea is indeed his doing. Furthermore, since Jonah has informed them that he is a fugitive from his

God, these poor sailors can only suspect the worst—this god is angry; and he will surely punish his man by sinking the ship with all hands.

The notion of an angry god who will unerringly work his retribution upon hapless humans is thoroughly ingrained in these men. They haven't the slightest doubt that an offended god must be appeased by some sort of sacrifice. The only question is the nature of the sacrifice. They now know that that sacrifice must involve Jonah, but how? So they ask him what they can do to him that will appease his god's anger so that "the sea may quiet down for us" (verse 11, RSV). But when he informs them that it will require a human sacrifice, they make a collective gulp and quickly go back to rowing. "Nevertheless, the men rowed hard to bring the ship back to land, but they could not" (verse 13, RSV). Now they are tired and truly terrified. What will this capricious sea god do to us if we kill his prophet?

It would be nice if we could say that Jonah's willingness to be sacrificed came from a truly repentant heart. A bit later it becomes clear that Jonah's decision in the boat was driven not by self-effacement, but by resignation. He really believed God was wrong, but he could not in good conscience take the ship and its entire human cargo with him to the grave. That was too much, even for Jonah's tattered convictions. So he made it perfectly clear to them that, to save their lives, they must sacrifice his. But even in his sacrifice he comes across as less than heroic. He could have lessened the sailors' guilt by simply leaping over the side of the boat. But Jonah doesn't have the stomach for it, so he insists that the sailors throw him overboard. At great personal anguish they accede to his wishes after a fearful prayer to this god of the elements, that he will not hold them responsible for Jonah's sacrificial death: "O Lord, let us not perish for this man's life, and lay not on us innocent blood" (verse 14, RSV). The immediate response of a calm sea increased the awe of the sailors, who "feared the Lord exceedingly, and they offered a sacrifice to the Lord and made vows" (verse 16, RSV). Their reaction is not intended to convince us that the sailors had converted to an exclusive worship of the God of the Hebrews. There is every reason to believe that their belief in and worship of other gods continued. But their responses are intended to highlight the narrowness and bigotry of Jonah. While Jonah holds in contempt pagans in general and Assyrians in particular, these faceless pagans respond to Jonah, try to save his life, and, finally, "worship" his God. The picture of contrasting attitudes is clearly intentional.

"And the Lord appointed a great fish to swallow up Jonah; and Jonah was in the belly of the fish three days and three nights" (verse 17, RSV). A whale has been popularly linked with Jonah down through the centuries. That connection has been favored because something very large is required to ingest a man whole, and no other known sea creature seems to be a good match. However, it should be remembered that this was a God-prepared sea creature. In attempts to bolster the historicity of the story, interpreters have made numerous attempts to document instances of persons being swallowed by whales and surviving. However, outside of this incident, "there is no known instance of a man being swallowed by a fish and being later cast forth alive" (James D. Smart, in *The Interpreter's Bible,* gen. ed. George A. Buttrick [Nashville: Abingdon Press, 1956], Vol. VI, p. 874). This miracle is only one of several that make up the Jonah story; but since it has the highest rating on the "incredible" scale, it is the one most often remembered and retold.

Chapter 2 of this story brings to light a different problem. The scene it presents is most unusual. "Then Jonah prayed to the Lord his God from the belly of the fish, saying . . ." (verses 1, 2, RSV). But what follows is a poetic hymn of praise. A cry for deliverance, an impassioned confession, an appeal for forgiveness, all would fit the context. But a hymn of praise? It just doesn't seem to fit the occasion. At that point there is not a hint of deliverance, yet the statement is made, "I called to the Lord, out of my distress, and he answered me" (verse 2, RSV). Would he really say that while the "weeds were wrapped about my head" (verse 5)? Furthermore, not only is it written in the meter of typical Hebrew poetry, in contrast with the other three chapters of narrative, but several of the phrases can be found verbatim in Psalms 18, 31, 42, 50, and 69. Admittedly Jonah could have recited several of the psalms while languishing among the digestive juices of the fish, but it was surely an unlikely environment for such noble and creative reflecting.

A more likely suggestion is that his prayer from the "belly of the fish" took actual form sometime after the fact. Clearly the entire story was put into written form after the fact, so it is reasonable to conclude that the poetic hymn, likewise, was put together when the "weeds" were no longer "wrapped about my head" (verse 8). The view that the chapter was written in retrospect is strengthened by such phrases as "when my soul fainted within me I remembered the Lord" (verse 7) and "what I have vowed I will pay" (verse 9, RSV). Accordingly, it seems reasonable to conclude that sometime after the fish had deposited him back on dry land, after he had had time to dry off, collect his thoughts, and reconstruct his past few days, some deep soul-searching would have been in order. In that setting it is easy to imagine Jonah agonizing over how best to put into words what he had experienced. It is also not hard to imagine that psalms of praise for deliverance sprang to his mind as he played and replayed the terror of what he had thought was a long-drawn-out death, but instead turned out to be an unforgettable preview of death. His reverie ends with the acclamation "Deliverance belongs to the Lord!" (verse 9, RSV). It's as if God has brought him back from the dead; back from a far country, back to his God. He has learned his lesson. He is now ready to take up the mission he had tried so hard to escape.

"Then the word of the Lord came to Jonah the second time" (Jonah 3:1, RSV). It is a phrase that tempts one to spiritualize and moralize and even dramatize. "Isn't it wonderful that God gave Jonah (and, of course, us) a second chance?" A second chance? Is that all we get—two chances? To make too much of the phrase is to make too little of His grace. The theme of Jonah, and of so many of these stories, is the seemingly endless pursuit of Heaven's Hound. He doesn't call just once or twice, but again and again. God has already stepped into Jonah's path more than twice. He called him, He sent a storm to flush him out of his hiding place, He controlled the outcome of the sailors' lot-casting, He prepared a special fish and told it where to vomit. The lesson is obvious—the word of the Lord comes repeatedly. His persistence is condescension not to our complacency, but to our humanness. And it happens because that is simply one of the ways grace is actually spelled.

So after the most harrowing week of his life, Jonah is now ready to say yes to God's second invitation to service. Or so it appears. But the text says that he went to Nineveh "according to the word of the Lord" (verse 3), and it soon becomes apparent that the word of the Lord and the will of Jonah are still miles apart. Surprisingly, Jonah's narrow notions of nationalism survived the sojourn in the fish. True, he "arose and went to Nineveh" (verse 3, RSV), but it was a reluctant, perfunctory obedience. His later anger over God's forbearance and forgiveness of the Assyrians (verse 2) makes clear that Jonah's disdain for non-Israelites and hatred of the Ninevites were still very much in place. Consequently, his cryptic message of doom to Nineveh may have had a nice ring to it in his ears. But when he began to see the responsiveness of the people to his message, his bigoted heart began to sink. Whether or not God permitted Jonah to include any message of hope in his preaching, he held out none. His message spoke only of doom and destruction. No repentance/forgiveness option was offered. Accordingly, when the king of Nineveh called on all the people to repent and change their evil ways, part of his reason was "Who knows, God may yet repent and turn from his fierce anger, so that we perish not?" (Jonah 3:9, RSV). This wording suggests that Jonah offered them no alternative to their imminent destruction.

What followed were surely the longest 40 days of Jonah's life. Presumably he had to get the word around to "an exceedingly great city, three days' journey in breadth" (verse 3, RSV). Just how large "three days' journey in breadth" is has been vigorously debated. If the text meant it would take three days to walk straight across it, that would suggest it was some 50 to 75 miles across—a considerable exaggeration for any known city of that era. The text could mean that it would take three days of walking up and down the primary streets for Jonah to get completely across the city with his message. It could also refer "not to the diameter of the city proper but to the complex of villages which clustered about Nineveh" (Edward J. Young, *An Introduction to the Old Testament* [Grand Rapids: William B. Eerdmans Pub. Co., 1969], p. 263). In any case, his extended month of preaching bad news to the largest city he had ever seen was hardly a pleasant experience. I can imagine with some relish announcing to a city that in 40 days each person would be a $2 million lottery winner. No one thinks ill of the bearer of good news. But the bearer of bad news is often treated with scorn, even if the individual had nothing to do with why the news was bad. So although the repentance spread rapidly and was apparently genuine while the 40 days progressed and their future remained uncertain, the people probably didn't invite Jonah home for supper. Even though they came to believe his message, Jonah couldn't have been well liked. And day after day, that would get to you.

"And the people of Nineveh believed God; they proclaimed a fast, and put on sackcloth, from the greatest of them to the least of them" (verse 5, RSV). What a rebuke to Israel in general and Jonah in particular. The responsiveness of Nineveh and the intransigence of Israel are key themes of the story. For years a variety of prophets had given warning after warning to wandering, wayward Israel. Their spiritual drift had included everything from arrogance of the rich over the poor to bribery (Amos 5:12) to outright idolatry. Prophetic calls for reform were often met with responses that varied from cool indifference to hostile rejection. The contrasting response of the Assyrians sounded a very loud message to Jonah and to Israel.

Nor should the lesson be lost on contemporary spiritual Israelites. Attitudes of exclusivism are hardly limited to Israel of old. In fact, spiritual arrogance may still, on occasion, raise its ugly head. Notions that God has been exclusive in His calling are frequently ingrained and surprisingly stubborn. It is one thing to feel that God has led us along every step of our spiritual journey. It is quite another to feel that other people *who are not where I am on the journey* are unbelievers who are surely headed for the fires of hell. Similar is the thought: *given time, all other true believers should eventually get to where I am on the journey.* But that attitude suggests that we should be using the word *destination,* not *journey.* In other words, if we feel that we have arrived at a spiritual or even doctrinal destination, that our journey/progress is now ended, we just may be in danger of slipping into Jonah's boat of exclusivity. It was during Jonah's time that God picked at the scab of Israel's narrow nationalism with the probing questions "Are you not like the Ethiopians to me, O people of Israel? . . . Did I not bring up Israel from the land of Egypt, and the Philistines from Caphtor and the Syrians from Kir?" (Amos 9:7, RSV). It was as if they were pained to think of their God as large and universal. They preferred Him to be small and tribal and all theirs. Similarly, it just might cause us considerable discomfort were we to paraphrase the text: "Did I not bring Adventism from New England, Protestantism from Germany, Catholicism from Rome, and Islam from Medina?" Are we more comfortable with a small denominational god or the God whose grace reaches out to all nations?

But Jonah was not of a mind to pick up on the message. The repenting Ninevites "displeased Jonah exceedingly, and he was angry" (Jonah 4:1, RSV). His near-death experience and the attendant miracles of his trip had changed him not at all. "Is not this what I said when

I was yet in my country? That is why I made haste to flee to Tarshish; for I knew that thou art a gracious God and merciful, slow to anger, and abounding in steadfast love" (verse 2, RSV). But he might as well have added, "But those are the traits You are to manifest toward Israel, not toward pagans. You belong to us, not them." It is with difficulty that each generation learns that it is not enough to be a recipient of God's grace. After His grace hits its mark in our lives, we are to be God's hands to reach out to others, His voice to speak out to others, His feet to travel to the despicable Ninevites of this world. The early Christian church certainly had to relearn this truth. You can almost hear the shock in Peter's voice when, as the Cornelius story unfolded, he said, "Truly I perceive that God shows no partiality, but in every nation any one who fears him and does what is right is acceptable to him" (Acts 10:34, 35, RSV). And a little later the Christian authorities were constrained to blurt out, "Then to the Gentiles also God has granted repentance unto life" (Acts 11:18, RSV). It makes you wonder if they had ever read the story of Jonah.

But what about Jonah's unequivocal prediction that Nineveh was about to be toast? Does God mean what He says, or are all His pronouncements negotiable? The answer lies in the nature of conditional prophecy. It is true that some conditional prophecies have *if* clauses that make the conditional aspect very clear. But there are unqualified phrases that sound unequivocal yet may have a hidden condition. Most Christians understand that, according to Romans 3:19, the whole world stands guilty and condemned before God. There are no *ifs* or *but if* clauses. However, there are *ifs* and *but ifs* elsewhere, so much so that even Paul, who stated that all humans are lost, understood that that conclusion is quickly altered "if we confess our sins." On that condition, God "is faithful and just to forgive us our sins, and to cleanse us from all unrighteousness" (1 John 1:9). So, although all are lost (Rom. 3:19), all unrighteousness can be cleansed. Just so with Jonah's prophecy of doom for sinful Assyrians. Their sinful ways will surely doom them. But if . . . just maybe . . . It was because Jonah understood well the issue of conditional prophecy that he had fled in the first place. He knew God's forgiving nature would alter the outcome if conditions changed. "The unstated condition was presupposed in the very character of God as a God of mercy and compassion" (*Seventh-day Adventist Bible Students' Source Book,* p. 766). God works *with* changeable people, not in spite of them. Thus, on occasion, He issues His ultimatum; people take notice and change; whereupon, the conclusion gets adapted to the changed situation. Forgiven sinners need not be destroyed. And in this case, it is especially significant because the people forgiven were considered the least likely to respond, and also considered by Israel to be the least worthy of being forgiven.

The final episode in the Jonah saga is as unattractive as the first. He began with an incident of opposition and he ends with much the same. First, he did everything he could think of to avoid giving the message. Then, after reluctantly delivering his message throughout the city and noticing that the people responded positively to his message, he proceeded to express his bitter opposition to God's grace for such unworthy people. But he cannot bring himself to walk off into the sunset without knowing exactly how things are going to turn out and "what would become of the city" (Jonah 4:5). Clearly he clings to the hope that his intuition will be wrong and that the city will, in fact, be destroyed. It is not the attitude expected of a prophet. How long he spent actually preaching and how long he spent watching from the hillside for the fire to fall are not spelled out, but no matter the time, Jonah is determined to wait it out. His building of a protective lean-to is evidence of his fixed frame of mind and his fear that this story is not going to end the way he thinks it should. And as Jonah waits, the Lord constructs some final confrontations with which to afflict/teach Jonah.

First, a fast-growing plant, probably a castor-oil plant (James D. Smart, in *The Interpreter's Bible* [Nashville: Abingdon Press, 1956], Vol. VI, p. 894), sprang up in just the right place and rapidly covered Jonah's lean-to, providing him with much-appreciated shade. Now he can watch in comfort while his enemies die. The plant is cool, literally; the plant must be protected; the plant is his friend. But the plant and his comfort are short-lived—they die quickly, in only one day. The God who can direct the swimming patterns of a giant fish can also direct the squiggly travels of a lowly cutworm. It makes breakfast of the crucial root, and the shade plant withers rapidly under the desert sun. The heat rises, and with it, Jonah's anger. He can take no more. He is so angry he just wants to die. His sympathy for his own comfort and for the lowly plant, in which he had invested nothing, outstripped any such feelings for the Ninevites. But God said to Jonah, "Do you do well to be angry for the plant?" And he said, "I do well to be angry, angry enough to die" (verse 9, RSV). "You have betrayed me, and now I will always be viewed as a false prophet. My reputation is in tatters." And God answers, "But, Jonah, if it is your reputation versus several thousand lives, what do you think the decision must be?" The contrast between Jonah's animosity and God's compassion for both Nineveh and Jonah is striking. God had used Jonah as His "hound" to track down the Ninevites and invite them back. They had responded, and His forgiving grace came into wonderfully sharp focus. But, in an unusual twist, Jonah was not only the hound sent after the lost people of Nineveh; he was, at the same time, the lost prophet of Israel, the object of Heaven's invisible Hound. In fact, no fugitive exemplifies more graphically the relentless pursuit or the many disguises of the Hound of Heaven than Jonah. If we look at each confrontation as a call back to the path of faith, how many calls did this one man receive? He fled, but the Hound materialized in the form of a life-threatening storm. Then the terrified and superstitious sailors cast lots, and the outcome bore the imprint of the Hound. Jonah's death plunge into the sea was interrupted by Heaven's Hound in the form of a giant fish that transported him to just the right beach. Then there was the shady bush and the worm, the withering winds off the desert, and then the lecture. The Hound has many faces—all used for one purpose—to track and confront wandering humans, not to condemn and bring guilt, but to find and bring home.

Was this hunt successful? The story ends abruptly with God's probing appeal to Jonah's logic and to his twisted priorities. The Lord said, "You pity the plant, for which you did not labor, nor did you make it grow, which came . . . in a night, and perished in a night. And should not I pity Nineveh, that great city?" (verse 10, RSV). The abruptness of the ending is not a flaw. We focus on Jonah and often wonder if he made it all the way back to the place of trust in and peace with God. But the purpose of the book is not to answer that question. With God's question the lesson is completed, the purpose fulfilled. The wideness of His grace has dramatically exposed the narrowness of Jonah's view. The lesson is so obvious that no labored application is necessary. Whether or not Jonah learned it is not the most important question. Whether or not we have learned it—now, that is the important question.

CHAPTER 10

PETER:
Back From the Brink

THE RECORD ISN'T CLEAR ABOUT which brother was the elder, but it is clear about which one talked more. It wasn't Andrew. In fact, Andrew almost comes across as part of the background for the real events. Maybe that's one reason his introduction is so unusual. His noisy brother, Simon, had a reputation for being first on the scene, the first to be introduced, and always the first to speak. So their very first introduction in opposite positions is intriguing. For the first and last time in Scripture, Andrew comes into focus before Simon.

But first let's set the scene. New Testament Palestine was a hotbed of frustrated nationalism. With numerous Old Testament promises of greatness and glory constantly ringing in their heads, Jews everywhere chafed under humiliating reminders that their glory was all in the past. All greatness now was spelled R-o-m-e, and the Jewish people were powerless to do anything about it. There was a constant "in your face" attitude by the Roman presence and power. Only one hope remained—the Messiah. He will come, and when He does, those needling infidels will finally get their comeuppance, and Jews will get back their self-esteem. He will see to it that no Jew will ever again go hungry or be demeaned in any way. In their synagogue Sabbath schools Jewish boys and girls learned well those memory verses that promised beautiful things and a powerful Deliverer in Israel's future. The brothers Andrew and Simon could repeat them all.

Now the brothers are adults and busy with their lives as hardworking fishermen. Their hands were calloused, and their hearts were heavy. The rope nets toughened hands, and the delay of their dreams saddened hearts. Would the Messiah come in their lifetime, or would they, like so many generations before them, go to dusty Palestinian graves, frustrated and humiliated? They often argued the question, and all kinds of suggestions flooded the marketplace of ideas. Some of their friends still believed that violent guerrilla tactics were the only means of success against the godless Romans. Others railed against creeping worldliness, and constantly asserted that if enough Jews were completely committed to God, the Messiah would come down in power and throw out the Romans. Some time back, a zealot had led a group of devout followers up a local mountain to watch, while God flattened all the fortresses of the Romans and drove them from Jerusalem. But alas, it was all for naught. Instead, Roman soldiers attacked the group, killing several, and the rest had to flee for their lives.

But surely those promises of power to the true believers were not all lies. God had not misled or forgotten His people. But when and how?

For Andrew and Simon, the answer to those questions could hardly have come in a more surprising form. The brothers were not together at the time—probably a common situation. Andrew was with his good friend John, listening to the latest and most exciting lay preacher, a man named John the baptizer. He was exciting because he kept goring the ox of Pharisaism by vigorously preaching unorthodox ideas and baptizing with no official credentials. Andrew and John liked to listen to him because he was unconventional and because he didn't seem to mind puncturing the windbags of the leaders' stuffed shirts. Then one lazy afternoon (at 4:00 most Palestinian afternoons feel lazy), almost incidentally, John the baptizer looked up and casually remarked, "Oh, here He is now—the Lamb of God" (see John 1:36). But it wasn't supposed to be like this. This was too incidental. You mean the Deliverer of God's people can come strolling onto the scene, feet actually touching the same dirt path we walk, wearing worn sandals, and looking for all the world like just another Galilean? What's wrong with this picture? There should at least be a thunderclap and a puff of smoke—preferably a miracle or two for verification. The day before, a faceless voice had identified the Messiah for John (verse 33), but he was the only one who seemed to know what it all meant. Later even he would have some doubts. How could the others know for sure? It would take some time.

Maybe it was a good thing that John's admirers had gotten used to hearing unorthodox ideas, because this new acquaintance, whom John had called the Lamb of God, also seemed to specialize in the unexpected. The second day of their meeting (verse 35), Andrew and his friend John (Zebedee's boy, not the baptizer) decided to follow Jesus home to see if they could get a little more perspective on the man as Messiah. They needed to see Him away from the public, as they had a lot of ideas to sort out. They didn't tell Him what they were doing; they just whispered their plan to each other and began following Him. When He noticed them back there and asked their intentions, they stammered out something about where His house was, and He invited them home. They never revealed what they saw, but something about that visit made very deep impressions. In fact, their lives would never be the same. There must be something very special about going home with Jesus. Most of us have visited Him on occasion, but maybe we haven't stayed long enough. In any case, the next thing that happens is that Andrew and John find their brothers and invite them to come and see what they have seen.

We don't know what happened when John introduced his brother James to Jesus, partly because the record of the introductions is anxious to tell us about Andrew and Simon. The brothers must have been widely known, if for no other reason than that Simon was such a dominant personality. Americans in recent times have seen how a man of fame can drag a brother, willing or not, into the limelight. First, there were Jimmy and Billy Carter. Later came Bill and Roger Clinton, and more recently, George W. and Jeb Bush. But long before, there were Simon and Andrew. I wouldn't want to press the analogy very far, but in each case both brothers have wide name recognition, but one brother seems to stand on a different level of the playing field.

Accordingly, Simon was not in the habit of doing much that his brother told him. Normally Simon did the telling. But on this occasion Andrew's announcement was too intriguing not to check out. Although messianic claims were not uncommon, this was the first time someone who was both a clear thinker and a relative had brought such news to Simon. He had to see for himself. Of course, that is always the way it should be with Jesus. People need to see for themselves. Convictions based on a very reliable source are usually good enough for reporting the news, but they rarely make solid Christians. "That which

. . . we have seen with our eyes, which we have . . . touched with our hands . . . we proclaim also to you" (1 John 1:1-3, RSV). Simon had to see with his own eyes and touch with his own hands. "He brought him to Jesus" (John 1:42). Andrew may have been the quiet one, but he must be credited with introducing Simon to the Savior. Later Simon will make enormous contributions to the Christian cause, but an important part of the credit must go to Andrew, the one whose first concern after meeting Christ was to introduce Him to his brother. What Simon saw and heard was completely unexpected.

Normally we meet and greet strangers in keeping with the social conventions of our time and place and age group. The options are many: "How do you do?" "Good morning." "How's it going?" "G'day, mate." Of course, Simon probably expected "Shalom," the ancient Hebrew greeting of peace. What he didn't expect was to be given a nickname. It must have seemed almost bizarre. Jesus, the total stranger, said, "So you are Simon. I'm going to call you 'Cephas'" (see John 1:42, RSV). We are so familiar with "Peter" as a proper name that the real significance of what Jesus did is lost on us. He didn't just change Simon's name to another name. It was not equivalent to saying, "I know your parents liked the name Simon, but I think Cephas sounds better." In the language of the day *Cephas* simply meant "rock." It was a noun or a descriptive adjective—rocklike—but not a name. The real intention of Jesus is better caught if we put it like this: "So you are Jim. I'm going to call you Bridge" (or Steel or some other inanimate thing). The point is, Cephas as a proper name was not what Jesus had in mind at all. John, who recorded the event, understood it perfectly; that's why he added the little explanation "which, when interpreted, means 'stone.'" Apparently John felt he needed to put everything into the Greek, so he came as close as he could by using the Greek equivalent to the Aramaic Cephas, and that was Petros. The actual Greek word for stone was Petra, but that is a feminine noun, and he couldn't use a feminine noun for a man, so he simply put a masculine ending on the feminine noun; hence, Petros. Had we kept the article, we might have stayed closer to the meaning. Simon the stone is probably very close to Jesus' meaning. But nicknames can do funny things—like completely eclipse the original name. With time and use, Simon's name evolved from Simon, to Simon *the* stone, to Simon Peter, to Peter. Incidentally, the terms gave no indication of the size or shape of the rock.

Jesus was making a prophetic statement about Simon's character development. It is interesting to note that throughout their time together Jesus rarely used his nickname when speaking to Simon. Nearly always He addresses him simply as Simon, or Simon son of John. Apparently Jesus never intended to replace the name Simon with the name Peter. Still, I can't think Simon's initial reaction was positive. Most of us develop some level of fondness for the name we grow up with. Even if we think our parents did us an injustice, if a stranger's first suggestion were a characterization that friends would soon develop into a nickname, we would probably think some uncomplimentary thoughts about that person. But if Simon was mystified by Jesus' unexpected characterization, no gospel account indicates that he resented Jesus' unusual approach. In fact, if Simon originally intended to come and scoff, he, like the others, quickly found himself caught up in fascination with his new acquaintance. One by one these first observers felt the impact of lingering in the presence of Jesus. Simon came to see, but stayed to learn and, eventually, to worship. One thing was soon clear: never could he go back to being just Simon the fisherman. From this day he would begin the tough task of becoming Simon Petros, of growing into his nickname. It would take some doing to become Simon the rock.

When Simon Peter comes into a scene, other people and details are often diminished. Not that he is a resented swaggerer. Persons with an overabundance of blandishments gradually isolate themselves until they walk pretty much by themselves. Not so with Peter. He was surrounded by friends, even when a large part of their fame and identity was simply that they were friends of Simon Peter. For example, shortly after the nucleus of Jesus' disciples was formed, while they were still unfamiliar with Jesus' habits of seeking secluded, private prayer, the revealing phrase in Mark 1:36 reads, "And Simon and those who were with him pursued him" (RSV).

He is the kind of man who, when he says, "I'm going fishing," is immediately joined by others who say, "We'll go with you" (see John 21:3, RSV). He spoke out often but was not resented, because his outbursts sprang from innocence, not arrogance. Furthermore, Peter's sentiments were often the sentiments of his friends and colleagues. On one occasion of healing, Jesus was surrounded by a jostling, boisterous crowd. When a woman reached out in faith and secretly touched His clothes, He asked her to identify herself (Luke 8:45). But given the crowd, His words "Who touched me?" seemed ludicrous. All the disciples thought so, but Peter was the only one with the nerve to voice their feelings. Luke puts it so plainly: "Peter [and those who were with him] said, 'Master, the crowds surround you and press in on you' " (verse 45, NRSV). They all said it to themselves, but only Peter blurted it out. "Master, isn't it a bit ridiculous to say 'Who touched Me,' when a whole crowd just did?" Sometimes when a fool rushes in, we are glad because we were about to do the same, but his brashness saves us the embarrassment. Maybe that was one reason the other apostles held no resentment for the ever-dominant Peter; they could count on him to be the first to test the waters of foolishness, and if he came up looking bad, they looked good by comparison.

There are many evidences of Peter's leadership position. Every time the apostles' names are listed (Mark 3:16, 17; Luke 6:14; Acts 1:13), Peter's is always first. The lists vary the order of the other names, but they never vary on the first one. The order of the names is not alphabetical, nor is it the chronological order of when they accepted the invitation of Jesus. For most of the list the reason for the order is hard to determine, but scholars agree that Peter was first because he was the acknowledged spokesman and leader. On three intense occasions, when Jesus wanted a small, intimate support group, He picked the same three, and they are always listed in the same order: "Peter and James and John" (Mark 5:37; Matt. 17:1; Mark 14:33). One of those occasions was the Mount of Transfiguration. All three disciples were a bit baffled by what they had seen, but that didn't keep Peter from speaking up. Another of those occasions was the Garden of Gethsemane, when Jesus hoped in vain for their prayer support. "He came and found them sleeping; and he said to Peter, 'Simon, are you asleep? Could you not keep awake one hour?' " (see Mark 14:37, NRSV). Jesus spoke directly to Peter, not because he was the only one sleeping, but because he was the representative of all the others.

One problem in being a leader is that your high visibility advertises flaws as well as talents, gaffes as well as gifts. Peter had plenty of both. His impetuousness leaps out of several incidents. He was an intense man who was not the kind to sit quietly and watch things develop and then, after carefully weighing the options, cautiously speak and move ahead. He was a man of impulsive action who spoke first and weighed options second. If there were consequences, he would deal with them if and when he had to. Early one morning an exhausted Peter brought his boat to shore after a futile night of fishing and proceeded to clean and wash his nets. In spite of the early hour, a crowd had already gathered to hear some words of guidance from Jesus. As the crowd swelled and backed Jesus into the edge of the lake, he borrowed Peter's boat for a platform and continued His morning devotional. When the service ended, Jesus suggested to Peter that they might as well push out a ways and bring in some fish for breakfast. Peter has just spent a wearisome night on these very waters with no success. For the past hour or so, he has been getting his nets all ready for their next night of fishing, and isn't keen on the idea of throwing the nets back into empty waters. Besides, every Galilean fisherman knew that nighttime was the best fishing time. Jesus was a lot of great things, but He was a carpenter, not a fisherman. Peter casually informs Him that it will be a lot of work for nothing. But Jesus prevails, and a reluctant and condescending Peter hauls out his cleaned and carefully stowed nets once more. The result astounds but does not silence him. It will take a great deal more than a little humble pie to make him speechless. "Depart from me; for I am a sinful man, O Lord" (Luke 5:8). From a position of confidence in his professional opinion he falls at Jesus' feet and admits that his stubborn pride was just another name for sin. True to his impulsive nature, he rushes, in a heartbeat, from a posture of assurance to facedown surrender. You've got to admire a man who doesn't waste time riding the fence of indecision.

Much later it happened again. A few details differed, but the outcome was similar enough to call it "same song, second verse." As they approached shore after a futile night of fishing, Jesus, not recognizable in the fog, called out to them and asked if they had caught anything. It was not the kind of question an unsuccessful fisherman likes to answer, let alone holler to a stranger on shore for lots of other ears to hear. But since the stranger had used the friendly word *children* (John 21:5), they were polite enough just to say no, instead of "Mind your own business." He then told them to try one more time on the other side of the boat. *Yeah, sure, like eight feet to the right will make a big difference.* But they were frustrated just enough that one more empty net wouldn't be a big deal. Except this time the net came up with enough fish to make the entire night of work worthwhile. The sudden work of hauling in the fish eclipsed the importance of the stranger on the shore, except for intuitive John. He quickly concluded that only Jesus could give them that kind of instruction. When he mentioned his suspicion to Peter, Peter dived into the lake and swam the 100 yards to shore so that he would be the first to greet the Lord. But it was a big job to pull up a net completely full of fish, so when Jesus asked them to bring in a few fish for breakfast Peter went back aboard and helped haul in the huge catch. He must have often exasperated his friends, but they had to admire how quickly he would act on his convictions.

His most famous act of brashness had a childish simplicity about it that endears him to many. I can easily imagine making the same request. Who wouldn't want to try walking on the water? True, the lake waters were still roiling from a storm, but that only heightened the excitement. But as so often happened, his reach exceeded his grasp, his actions raced ahead of his thoughts. "Lord, I'd love to try that. Would You allow me, just this once? I can't imagine what Ruth and the kids will say!" The boyish thrill briefly clouded his vision of the waves. As the boat got farther away his head cleared, and he "noticed the strong wind" (Matt. 14:30, NRSV). His faith in Jesus was suddenly replaced with sheer terror. What a familiar story. When we focus on Jesus, our trust in Him can conquer oceans of fear. On the other hand, when we shift our attention to the enormous phone bill or the troubled teenager, Jesus fades away, and we start sinking down into the waters of worry. But Peter's story here and elsewhere should give us encouragement. The patient Jesus is never out of earshot. No wind or wave is boisterous enough to drown out Peter's cry of desperation and faith, "Lord, save me!" Of course, a more focused faith would have kept his clothes dry, but the dripping-wet, sputtering Peter teaches us things about Jesus and forgiveness that a dry Peter could not. Since faith that falters in the face of fiery trial is the kind many of us know best, this story fits our situation again and again.

The point is that we erect pedestals for all the saints of old and carefully place their plaster likenesses high above us. Consequently, even their examples of failings or forgiveness seem always on a higher plane than ours. But their faith and their foibles were fleshy and fallible, exactly like ours. This is why Peter is such a favorite, because we strongly suspect he will be saved; yet he presents us with such a wide variety of just plain human traits. Such as talking when he had no idea what he was saying.

It happened on the Mount of Transfiguration. Moses and Elijah had appeared with words of encouragement for Jesus as He looked ahead toward the cross. When they disappeared, Peter, James, and John, senses dulled by fatigue and sleep, weren't at all sure what they had seen or what it all meant. James and John knew better than to open their mouths and let stupidness come out. But Peter had no such reservation. There must be some appropriate word for this auspicious occasion, if only he could figure out what it was. Finally he could stand the silence no longer and babbled, "Master, it is good for us to be here; let us make three dwellings, one for you, one for Moses, and one for Elijah" (Luke 9:33, NRSV). If he was planning to set up camp, he must have figured he and his two friends would just sleep on the ground. According to Luke, they were just words with no rational thought behind them. He adds the terse footnote, "Not knowing what he said." It wasn't a sin; it was just human. Like all of us, Peter stood in need of daily grace and patience as, throughout his entire life, he continued to mature and grow and overcome flaws.

Throughout his years with Christ, Peter rarely strayed far from the path of faith. Once he committed himself to the Master, he was not like David, who strayed far into forbidden territory. In this respect many struggling Christians today can identify with Peter. Like him, their problems are not blatant immorality or rebellion, but repetition of "little" sins and a nagging sense that their faith is just not dynamic enough to get them to the kingdom. It's true that for Peter, the Hound of Heaven didn't have to go sniffing deep into the thicket of apostasy to find him; at least, not until late in his relationship with Jesus. Of course, that in itself is troubling. After a few years of fairly small bumps in his faith development, what do we make of a major denial when he should have been well up the ladder of sanctification?

Matthew 26:33-35 tells the story of that last night of opportunity. Never again would Jesus need the prayers and moral support of His disciples as He would need them this night. In a secluded spot of a familiar garden He is about to agonize over a life-or-death decision—for a universe. After this night a most intense part of His trial would be over, and He earnestly asks them, not once, but three times, to pray with Him. It is the only time in His ministry that He makes such a request. His very being shudders before the awesome struggle He is going through, and "He came to His disciples with a yearning desire to hear some words of comfort. . . . He longed to know that they were praying for Him and for themselves" (*The Desire of Ages,* pp. 687, 688). But instead he found them sleeping. While "the fate of humanity trembled in the balance" (*ibid.,* p. 690), Peter and his friends slept.

Jesus had earlier tried to warn them of the seriousness of this night by informing them, "You will all fall away because of me" (Matt. 26:31, RSV). Was it only a prediction, or an attempt to put them on the defensive so their guard would be up and they would be prepared? It's hard to know for sure, but the one man who had given a vigorous defense of himself was Peter. "Though they all fall away because of you, I will never fall away" (verse 33, RSV). So having gone on record with such a ringing testimonial, Peter was now perfectly set up for his most humiliating and ignominious defeat. He was about to stumble openly and publicly off the path of faith and deep into the brambles of denial and apostasy.

First he appeared to back up his assertion of loyalty, but it was largely bravado and show. When the crowd of soldiers, Jewish collaborators, and onlookers came shuffling with their lamps into the quiet garden to arrest Jesus, Peter ran among the crowd, unsheathed his small sword, and swung at the first man he could reach—who turned out to be not a soldier at all, but an unarmed servant of the high priest. What Peter was hoping to accomplish is not at all clear, but it was probably not simply to de-ear a harmless man. In any case, Jesus' intervention and miracle of healing in His own hour of extremity probably saved Peter from arrest, if not execution. As perceived threats to their safety increased, Matthew, who was probably guilty himself, gives the sad comment "Then all the disciples deserted him and fled" (verse 56, NRSV). He didn't say, "All but Peter." Matthew does add, however, that "Peter followed him afar off" (verse 58). But it was not so that he could come to His aid, but only "to see the end."

It was while watching all the tragic "end" events that Peter really struck out. First, after hearing Jesus' earnest plea for help, Peter had slept. Strike one. Then he tried his sword before fleeing. Strike two. Finally, in spite of a direct warning that he would deny his Lord, he denied his Lord. Strike three. Maybe it was the unexpected direction from which the temptation came. It was just an offhand remark of a young girl. How could he have guessed this was the really big temptation? He was expecting a direct attack from a known enemy. It's a lesson we are all exasperatingly slow to learn—temptations surprise us. We look right, and they hit us from the left. They sneak into our activities from sources we can hardly admit—the suggestion of a friend, the sudden bad example of a role model, the belligerence of a child, the swerve of a bad driver on our way to church. Maybe the problem is in watching for temptations, instead of watching the Lord. In Peter's big test he had more than one opportunity to catch himself, but he failed all three times. During the last time, the proof he offered was language the Bible writers felt was too inappropriate to print.

Then the rooster crowed, and the memory of Jesus' warning came flooding back into his mind. His own bellicose assertion that he would stand firm while the others denied their faith now rose like a specter of defeat and death. How could he ever come to terms with what he had done? It's one thing to miss an opportunity—another one will come along sooner or later. But once-in-a-lifetime opportunities are extremely rare. And this had been one. Never could Peter really make right what he had done. The one night Jesus needed human help and companionship, the one occasion Jesus was literally hurting, Peter could have helped by showing his loyalty and support. Instead, those who would inquire for all the rest of time would read how, at that most significant of all moments, he had cursed and sworn and looked the other way. The other followers just ran away and hid. Peter did worse: he went public with his lack of support—he advertised it to the world. The enormity of his failure fell in upon him quickly, and he ran from the scene.

As he stumbled through the night he replayed the scene dozens of times. He couldn't help remembering that time Jesus had asked them, "Who do men say that the Son of man is?" (Matt. 16:13, RSV). The other disciples had given the various speculations, but he, Peter, had noisily blurted out the conclusion they had often discussed among themselves: "You are the Christ [Messiah], the Son of the living God" (verse 16, RSV). To which the other disciples had all murmured some sort of "Yes, that's right; we all think that, Lord. Peter has spoken our sentiments exactly." But now his mind kept repeating to him the most recent testimonial from his lips: *No, you're very mistaken, I have no idea who He is, and I wish you'd keep your *&!+)*=%! opinions to yourself!* Peter was never a tentative person. He couldn't be subtle if he tried. Consequently, the volume of his denial was as great as his earlier expressions of belief. There are many ways to deny one's loyalty to Christ, but few of us have done it as publicly or as noisily as did Peter. How could he ever make it right again? Computers have an "undo" command. Never had Peter felt so intently the need of an "undo" key for his life. If only he could take it all back and start the night over. "Boys flying kites haul in their white-winged birds, but you can't do that when you're flying words."

What followed was the most awful weekend of his entire life. Hiding out for fear of attack is one thing. When your cause is just, you can actually do that with pride. But hiding out from friends you have betrayed not only destroys all pride, but shreds self-worth. What was that Jesus had said? "Simon, I'm going to call you rock"? Yeah, right. Rocklike indeed! No, the nickname was in fact turning into the verb of failure—he was truly petering out. Maybe what Jesus meant was not granite-like but something on the order of sandstone or pumice—some sort of crushable stone that easily changes its shape and texture. His huge failure caused him to look inside in ways he had never done. What he saw was depressing—all his previous proclamations of faith had turned to sand under the blow of one crucial temptation. He could hardly face himself, let alone his friends and Jesus.

One by one he reconnected with the other disciples. That was the easy part of his restoration. After all, none of them had shown courage. True, Peter's cowardice topped them all, but his volume and visibility usually did. As they now came back together, they must have looked like whipped pups, sheepishly sneaking out of their hiding places after a thunderclap. How haunting now were Jesus' words of warning that when the Shepherd was struck, the sheep would be scattered. They all felt humbled, but Peter felt terrible. More than the others he felt the fool because he had been so noisy with his earlier predictions of loyalty. Though it was by far the most serious mistake of his life as a disciple, none of his weak friends was about to hold it over his head. Besides, they had all become accustomed to his frequent contrition and readily accepted his most heartfelt "I'm sorry." They forgave him much more easily than he could ever forgive himself.

We are not privileged to listen in on his first words with Jesus after the denial. However, one bit of dialogue in John 21:15-19 gives us a glimpse of the postdenial relationship between them. They have just finished the breakfast Jesus made for them, and He is soon to leave them for good. Out of the blue He asks Peter if he loves Him "more than these" (verse 15)? Was it a sudden flashback to Peter's boast "Though all of them should deny you, I never will?" It seems so. But if it is, Peter doesn't take the bait. His answer is impressive for where it stops. He will say only, "Yes, Lord; you know that I love you" (verse 15, NRSV). He is not about to make any more pretentious comparisons between himself and them. So Jesus also drops the comparison part, but presses him a bit more by repeating the question about his love—twice! So Jesus gives Peter three opportunities to publicly express his love. Each time Peter offers no bravado, no flamboyant overstatement. In fact, there is almost a reluctance to say much at all. His comment "Lord, . . . you know that I love you" (verse 17, NRSV) is almost like saying, "You already know it, so why do I have to say it?" It's as if he doesn't want to go on record for fear he might not live up to his word. Some difference from his earlier unsolicited brag: "They may all fall away, but I never will!" The man and his attitude have changed.

So what are we to make of Simon Peter—this mixture of solid conviction and childish weakness, this combination of greatness and groveling, of stardust and mud? Had he finally, just before Jesus' ascension, grown into his nickname? Was he at last the rock Jesus said he would be? The answer would continue to be mixed. Perhaps Jesus never meant the term to be viewed as an all-or-nothing, before-and-after prediction. At least it's hard to find an event that once and for all turned Simon from soft putty into solid rock. Throughout the time of Jesus' ministry Simon repeatedly demonstrated some rocklike traits of commitment and leadership that were recognized and accepted by the 12. But as we have seen, his leadership activities were repeatedly interrupted by acts and words of foolishness.

In the early weeks and months after Jesus' ascension Peter clearly assumed his rocklike role of leadership. Shortly after Jesus left them, Peter took charge of things and was in the dominant position on that famous Pentecost when the Spirit came and the Christian church was born. He would continue to dominate the early Christian scene with numerous unflinching testimonials to the Messiah. At one point the power of his presence had grown to such legendary proportions that some folks thought even his shadow had healing properties (Acts 5:15). Much later, however, when pressure between groups of leaders built up, he took a compromising position of prejudice against Gentiles and was publicly rebuked by Paul (Gal. 2:14). Apparently you don't have to be perfect to be a rock in the church.

But the question lingers: How could Jesus, on the first day of their meeting, look at Peter and even think rock? The answer lies in the concept of potential. This must be one of the most crucial reasons the Hound of Heaven is so persistent in His searches. He hunts down lost souls because of His craving to see us reach our potential. He sees what we are capable of, once He leads us out of the thicket. We humans are not very good at this. It seems to be hard for us to allow people a chance to grow. We are better at remembering where they have been than where they are going. "Isn't he the one who got into trouble a couple of years ago and had to . . . ?" "Isn't she the single parent who never wants to tell us why her husband . . . ?" We look at a human and see their past. The Lord looks at a human and sees their future.

Not only does the Lord see our great potential; He wants to help us get there. One time when Jesus was talking to Peter He said, "Simon, Satan wants to get hold of you so that he can sift you like wheat, but I have prayed for you that your faith might not fail" (see Luke 22:31). What incredible encouragement for Peter and for us. As with Peter, our wishy-washy past casts a shadow of doubt over our future success. Not only that, but Satan is out to put us through his sieve. Our prospects look grim. But Jesus, the Son of God, affects everything. He looks into our past and sees failure. He looks into our future and sees more of the same. He should flee from such lost causes; but instead He forgives them, adopts them, and empowers them.

He does ask one thing of us: that we follow Him. He willingly invades our thicket of despair, but He wants to lead us out, not drag us out. One day as He looked into Peter's difficult future and described certain aspects of his death, Jesus concluded with the simple instruction "Follow Me." Moments later, when Peter asked Jesus about John's future, Jesus replied that that was not Peter's concern. "Your concern," Jesus repeated, "is very simple: follow Me." He's promised to handle the tough parts. All we have to do is follow His lead.

CHAPTER 11

JUDAS:
Over the Brink

A LONE FIGURE MOVED STEADILY down the narrow street, his sandals making a *flack-flack-flack* on the cobblestones. The quiet of the night made his footfalls reverberate like thunder in his ears. Overhead, the Passover moon was full, but the sky was pockmarked with odd-shaped clouds that skittered across the black velvet, periodically swallowing the moon. The man's step was sure and determined. He knew his destination, and there was no hesitation in his getting there. Something, however, suggested a note of fear. He attempted a quiet whistle, but it came out dry and breathy, and he quickly gave it up. In another couple of hours his name, Judas, would be forever linked to the most heinous act of treachery the world has ever known. That name was about to be tarnished more than any name in human history. But by what route had he traveled to this terrible destination?

The biblical account is sketchy at best. Some see him first appearing in the mysterious, nameless scribe who, in Matthew 8:19, came unsolicited and offered his services to Jesus. "Teacher, I will follow you wherever you go" (NRSV). If that was Judas, he was met with the sobering rejoinder "Foxes have holes and birds of the air have nests; but the Son of Man has nowhere to lay his head" (verse 20, NRSV). It was not the kind of response that would create a desire to join the club, let alone inspire confidence in such a leader. "Judas, feel free to join our little circle of homeless people." "Well, on second thought . . ." In Matthew's account the incident occurs immediately after a series of miracle healings that had resulted in "great crowds around him" (verse 18, RSV). Also, the previous chapter gives the concluding statement of the Sermon on the Mount: "The crowds were astonished at his teaching, for he taught them as one who had authority, and not as their scribes" (Matt. 7:28, 29, RSV). In that setting it is not surprising that a person would want to join the inner circle of such a leader. But Jesus is quick to rebuff any who are attracted solely by surface appearances of success. Jesus seemed to say, "Don't try to do the right thing if it is for the wrong reasons. What you see is not what you're going to get."

Rounding a corner, his step quickened. He didn't want to miss his appointment with the authorities, even though his thoughts and feelings were more conflicted now than they had been for months. Just minutes earlier he had been in the upper room with Jesus and the 11 other disciples. Much to Judas' disgust, Jesus had taken a basin and towel and had acted very unprofessional, very unlike a Messiah. He had actually played the part of a common household servant and had gone all around the group washing their dirty feet (not nice clean feet from which clean socks and shiny shoes had just been removed) and drying them with a rag. The whole scene repulsed Judas. The joining together of the terms *servant* and *Messiah* was a bit too much for him to handle. That is, until Jesus gently touched his feet. When that happened, it was as if an invisible shudder ran through his body. A rush of sensations and thoughts overloaded his body and mind, but no words would form. Suddenly all his conclusions about Jesus seemed premature, maybe even wrong. As Jesus washed and dried Judas' feet, His movements were so deliberate they seemed to Judas to be in slow motion. A few minutes later Jesus had said, "Ye are clean, but not all" (John 13:10). Judas, who had always been quick to catch the double entendre, suspected the comment was meant for him, but his frozen expression leaked nothing to the 11. Heaven's Hound was nipping at his heels, but that could not, of itself, change the course of Judas' life or make his decision for him.

Following this were numerous awkward silences. Jesus seemed unusually burdened with heavy thoughts, and the 12 reflected His somber mood by a quietness they didn't really understand. After one such quiet time Jesus shattered the silence with the shocker "One of you will betray me" (verse 21, NRSV). Judas controlled his wince enough that the 11 still suspected nothing, but now he realized with some horror that

Jesus was on to him. But how much Jesus knew was suddenly the urgent question in Judas' mind. Again, the thought formed that he should just admit what he was planning and see if Jesus would do the right thing: proclaim His Messiahship and save Judas the embarrassment of being thought a betrayer. One thing was clear—he couldn't leave the room right now, as that would send a clear signal that he was the one Jesus had just referred to. At the same time, he could not connect the term *betrayer* to himself. No, that term was simply wrong. Rather, he had come up with a plan that he felt was truly win-win. He would assist the Sadducees in their goal of arresting Jesus in the dark so as to avoid any demonstrations of support by crowds. Jesus would then be forced to defend Himself and escape, which would immediately reveal His messianic power. Or, if that scene didn't happen, if Jesus actually allowed Himself to be taken captive by His enemies, then clearly He wasn't messianic material, and the sooner people saw the impotence of His power, the better for all concerned. In either case, the word would soon go out that it was Judas who had set the stage for the great revelation. No, the term *betrayer* was clearly the wrong term. Actually, Judas was about to help the Savior announce Himself as the "one who is about to redeem Israel." From either scenario, the fingers will point to Judas as the one who really "made it happen." Betrayer? No. Facilitator? Definitely.

Of course, the innocent 11 were completely bewildered and, one by one, inquired if they had somehow, through their own ignorance or naïveté, fallen for some treachery. "Lord, is it I?" was the question that started around the circle. The seating arrangement at the Passover meal for 13 people probably required a large U-shaped low table, around which the participants would be able to recline on their left elbows, enabling them to use their right hands for eating. Their feet would extend out at an angle from the table, thus making it easy for a servant to go around the outside, washing their feet. The place of the host would be at the bottom of the U. From this place Jesus had gotten up and had done the foot-washing work of a servant. The place of greatest honor would be right in front of the host and could be described as "lying close to the breast of Jesus," which was where John was (John 13:23, RSV). Also, there is the strong suspicion that as they took their seats, Judas was able to secure the place of the next-greatest honor, which was just behind Jesus (Leon Morris, *The Gospel According to John, New International Commentary on the New Testament* [Grand Rapids: Eerdmans Pub. Co., 1971], p. 626). Part of the Passover meal procedure included dipping pieces of bread in a sauce dish that usually served the three or four who could reach it. Peter, typically impatient with the slow-moving "Is it I?" routine, got the eye and ear of John, who was obviously closer to Jesus than Peter, and simply told John to ask Jesus who the guilty party was (John 13:24). After an awkward pause Jesus finally added, "It is one who is dipping in the dish with me" (see Mark 14:20, RSV). That narrowed down the possibilities to the three or four who could reach that particular dish, and also supported the notion that Judas was sitting close to Jesus, but it still did not reveal the actual culprit. Why was Jesus so agonizingly slow in His revelation of Judas' perfidy? Was He giving him opportunities to rethink His plan, to change his mind, to confess his sin?

But now the question had made its way around the circle toward Judas. Opportunities for confession had come and gone, and come and gone. Again we see demonstrated heaven's incomparable patience, even with those who set themselves on a course of rebellion. Finally Judas was forced to complete the circle of "Lord, is it I?" questions. According to John, even then Jesus spared him the harshest identification. Instead of a simple yes, or some other direct finger-pointing, Jesus took a more oblique tack. "'It is he to whom I hand this bread.' And having dipped the bread, he handed it to Judas" (see John 13:26, RSV). It was the last appeal, and what a pregnant moment it was. The silence at the table must have been deafening. Jesus, extending to Judas the piece of bread. Judas, hesitating, yet forced to reach out and accept the gift. All eyes are riveted on Judas, boring in with enormous question marks hanging in the dead stillness. Jesus must have looked him in the eye as He gave him the bread and with that look pierced his conscience with the final, unspoken question: "Judas, are you absolutely certain of what you are about to do?" In that instant Judas' very life hung quivering in the balance. Quickly and tragically the moment passed. Too many wrong decisions had built up a tough crust that Jesus' tender probe could not quite penetrate. Judas' decision stood firm, but as he hesitated, Jesus urged him to get on with it "quickly" (John 13:27). That statement did not mean that Jesus was eager for the betrayal to happen, but perhaps He simply wanted to get on with

His heartfelt instructions to the 11, which He could not do as long as Judas remained in the room.

The identity of the traitor is now clear, but not the extent of his treachery—at least not to the 11. Even when Jesus added the doleful words "What you are going to do, do quickly" (verse 27, RSV), the 11 had no clue. On occasion the disciples had shown a certain obtuseness of understanding, which once again revealed itself. "Some thought that, because Judas had the money box, Jesus was telling him, 'Buy what we need for the feast'; or, that he should give something to the poor" (verse 29, RSV). There are times that innocence or even ignorance (they sometimes run together) can be blissful. For the 11 this was surely one of those times. For another hour or so, how peaceful their minds must have been, compared to the minds of Jesus and Judas. Not to know can sometimes be the greatest gift. Their horror would come soon enough—but for a little while longer their cluelessness was their peace.

In contrast, it is hard to imagine the state of Judas' mind. He had left the table quickly, embarrassed by the exposure, but content in the knowledge that the other apostles didn't really know what was going on. Once outside, the evening air helped clear his conflicted mind. But John, a master of double meanings, added the cold and cryptic comment: "and it was night" (verse 30, RSV). For Judas, the dark of that night would never lift. Oh, he would see one more dawn, but the darkness of his soul was now sealed—not by God slamming his door of probation, but rather by his own choices and determination. It had taken months for him to flee into this condition of darkness, and Heaven's Hound had pursued him every step of the way. A year before this night, Jesus had fed thousands from a small lunch, and then keenly disappointed the crowds by refusing to yield to their clamor to proclaim Himself their provider-Messiah. Judas had been a key promoter of that idea, and on that occasion Jesus had lamented, "Did I not choose you, the twelve, and one of you is a devil?" (John 6:70, RSV). And John, reflecting on that thought many years later, added the clarification for any who might not understand, "He spoke of Judas the son of Simon Iscariot, for he, one of the twelve, was to betray him" (verse 71, RSV). In the last part of that phrase, "for he, one of the twelve, was to betray him," one can feel the emotional tie of John to Jesus and his absolute incredulity that one of the 12 could be involved in such treachery. It is as if he said, "And to think the betrayer was one of us! I can hardly believe it even now!"

But there had been another keen disappointment for Judas that helped nudge him toward the darkness that eventually enveloped him. It was at the time of the supper in the house of Simon the leper. Mary had lavishly "wasted" some very expensive perfume on Jesus' feet when water would have done the job quite well. On that occasion Judas was not alone in thinking that this act went considerably "over the top." Matthew, probably a participant in the criticism, did not try to protect himself but simply stated, "When the disciples saw it, they were indignant, saying, 'Why this waste?' " (Matt. 26:8, RSV). Furthermore, they didn't just think it and then keep it to themselves, since in His rejoinder Jesus said, "Why do you trouble the woman?" (verse 10, RSV). Obviously they made certain that she heard their murmuring. Jesus' restrained rebuke of the grumbling disciples contained the elemental truth that there are "impractical" values that transcend even the high-minded social concern for the poor. Here, Jesus pointed out, concern and compassion for the poor will always be an important aspect of our social atmosphere: "For you have the poor with you always, but me you do not have always" (see verse 11, RSV). In other words, Mary's act of worship, which included a sacrificial offering, presaged His sacrifice to come and would provide a powerful testimony to that event for all hearers for the rest of time. "Wherever this gospel is preached in the whole world, what this woman has done will also be told as a memorial to her" (see verse 13, RSV). A practical concern for careful money management and concern for the poor is important, but lavish, conspicuous acknowledgment of the forgiveness and acceptance of a Savior by an outcast is of even greater consequence.

"Why this waste?" The time would come when the disciples would remember with shame their terribly flawed assessment of her act—Matthew saw to that. But Judas would not allow himself time to remember, reflect, rethink, and eventually repent of his self-righteous, self-serving conclusion. Although Jesus' response on that occasion was directed at "the disciples" and not at Judas in particular, he nonetheless smarted at what he perceived to be a rebuke of his concept of the Messiah. It appears as a watershed experience for his conflicted mind, for the record indicates that he went directly from this event to the chief priests to pose the traitorous question " 'What are you willing to give me if I deliver Him to you?' and they counted out to him thirty pieces of silver" (see verse 14, RSV). Another decision had been made that would irrevocably lead him to that vale of darkness, which John worded with such succinct finality: "and it was night."

As he walked the streets, his clouded mind cleared, and his shaken resolve once again hardened. He looked up and realized that he was abreast of the entrance to the house of Caiaphas, the prearranged meeting place. He felt the leather money pouch on his side—only a few shekels left. But it would be fat again. The "authorities" had agreed to pay him, but only on completion of the deal, as they were highly skeptical that one of Jesus' inner circle would actually betray Him. But it wasn't the money that drove the devious decision of Judas. It was more his utter frustration with Jesus' style of servant leadership. Oh, the money would be a nice bonus, but the real benefit would be the revelation to all that Jesus was the Messiah of power for whom they'd all been waiting. Why Jesus had been so reticent to announce Himself was the mystery Judas couldn't solve. But he was sure that after tonight the mystery would be resolved one way or another. For if Jesus did not exert His power, if the unthinkable happened and He was actually taken into custody and imprisoned, then perhaps He was indeed a fraud; and if so, then that revelation was overdue. In that case, Judas would get the credit for one of the truly great exposés of history. Whatever the outcome, Judas figured he couldn't lose. Not only would his reputation be enhanced; he would also have 30 more pieces of silver.

But he chafed under the thought that Jesus had referred to him as a betrayer. He was convinced that that was the wrong word. Just a few days ago Jesus had raised Lazarus from the dead. Earlier He had walked on the water, calmed a storm, fed thousands with one little lunch. Surely such a man would not be affected by a small band of Roman soldiers. No, this was not a betrayal at all; it was simply a shrewd means of helping the humble Jesus tell the people who He really was. At last Jesus would assume the role of Messiah that Judas had always dreamed of. But therein lay the crux of the problem: it was Judas' dream, not God's.

It is good to dream. It is essential to a vibrant life to be able to ponder and envision what you would like to see take place. Such dreaming can bring excitement and a sense of freedom and liberation. It can start the creative juices flowing and bring about changes you never thought possible. But we must be careful to police our dreams, lest they take us captive and turn our freedom into slavery—slavery to the notion that my dream must become reality, not only for me, but for others as well. If we are ever to rise above the commonplace, if we are to experience life at a level above that of grinding boredom, we must dream, we must set up goals and expectations. At the same time, we must remember that our expectations are built upon human perceptions and thus may need to be adjusted when they come up against a different reality. This is especially true with regard to our expectations about God and how we think He should work for me and mine. Or perhaps it is parents or children who haven't lived up to the expectations we have created for them. But when establishing expectations for God or for parents or for children or for anyone else, we must be willing to acknowledge our flawed human perspective and be prepared to let things unfold in ways that may be quite unexpected. Otherwise, like Judas, we will be tempted to dig in our heels and insist that any development that isn't in my playbook must be rejected; every dream that goes unfulfilled is someone else's fault. But as the longest night in history wore on, Judas' carefully crafted plan would inexorably begin to unravel.

His meeting with the high priest proceeded pretty much as planned, except for one crucial detail—it was the wrong weekend! The Jewish authorities had made it very clear to Judas that the "transaction" was not to take place on any festival weekend, as they didn't want the crowds swelled by a lot of outsiders—especially visitors from up north where Jesus had spent most of His time. Consequently, they saw this timing as a disaster. Passover weekend always brought teeming crowds of visitors from throughout Palestine. The only festival that would create more exposure of "events" might be Pentecost week, as that high day was probably the best attended of all the Jewish festivals. Of course, astounding things would happen in Jerusalem that weekend as well, for it was not by chance that when the Holy Spirit came, creating the sound of a "rushing mighty wind" (Acts 2:2), there were enormous crowds that heard and responded. Men may work their mischief, but how often the timing is wrested from their hands by a more powerful hand. They could arrest Him and execute Him, but they would do it on His timetable, not theirs.

Caiaphas spoke: "So Judas, you surprise me—twice! First, I am pleasantly surprised that you are going through with it. After all, it isn't often that a student becomes so disenchanted with his rabbi that he is willing to betray him. We really didn't think you would actually pull it off." Judas winced. "And second, you surprise me by coming now! We made it very plain to you that we wanted no big crowds, and this weekend the place is crawling with them. Why now, Judas? Does it really have to be Passover weekend?"

"Yes, it does! I had no choice! Tonight wasn't my idea either, but He not only revealed that He knew I was up to something, He even told me to 'do it quickly.' I think He's known for a long time that I had talked with you about this. But when He pointed out my identity to the 11 others, I had to leave the room, and now I know I have to do this and we have to do it tonight!" For reasons he couldn't explain, Judas was seized with a sense of urgency. Having made his decision, an inner force seemed to compel him. Was his haste prodded because the quiet of his soul was being shattered by the braying of the Hound of Heaven? If so, the sooner the "act" could be finished, the sooner peace could descend. "He's probably telling the others right now. I'm not sure what they might try to do, but I know that we need to do this tonight. I know where He will go after their supper. You say you don't want a crowd. Well, He's not going to have a crowd with Him tonight, so you better follow my lead and grab Him while you can."

The high priest motioned for Judas to wait; he then stepped out the rear door and spoke quietly to a Roman soldier, who stepped off quickly into the night. Judas shifted from one foot to the other as the uncomfortable wait stretched on. After what seemed like hours Judas heard the approaching clomp-clomp of soldier boots on the hard-packed street. Caiaphas motioned Judas toward the door. As they stepped out into the darkness Judas was surprised at the number of soldiers that had gathered. *All these to bring in Jesus?* he thought to himself. He almost chuckled as he remembered the ease with which Jesus had once quieted a windstorm that had come roaring across Galilee. A whole garrison of soldiers would be no match. He was starting to feel smug again.

"Well, Judas, where to?" Suddenly it dawned on him that this band of soldiers was awaiting his command. He suddenly felt warm and powerful and courageous. His uncertainty of an hour ago was rapidly melting away. He knew the way to Jesus' favorite place of quiet rest, but given tonight's circumstances and his leadership role, he carried a torch. As they proceeded down through the Kidron Valley and over toward the Garden of Gethsemane, Judas finally felt good; he was in charge. I wonder if he was humming to himself something like "This little light of mine, I'm going to let it shine"? If so, he would soon be slinking out of the garden saying "Hide it under a bushel? Yes!" But for the moment he reveled in the thought that he no longer felt insignificant and anonymous. Perhaps he was saying, "Tonight is my night. After tonight, my name will be remembered." In fact, it suddenly dawned on him that, in a certain way, he was actually leading a crowd to Jesus. Later, when Jesus would break free from the arresting soldiers, would the crowd then acknowledge His power and accept Him? Might they actually become the first real converts to Christianity? Would Judas then be credited with the very first baptisms? One thing was clear in his mind: after tonight he would be famous. How true his prediction and how sad!

Judas led the motley group out through the city gate and down through the little valley where the brook Kidron trickled. As they were about to enter the secluded olive grove called Gethsemane, Judas instructed the officers, "Whomsoever I shall kiss, that same is he; take him, and lead him away safely" (Mark 14:44). But in his mind the thought kept popping up, "How can this band of men arrest and bind the One who has raised the dead?" Just then a large cloud slid over the moon, which added to the sense of foreboding that now spread among the soldiers. Someone grumbled about the danger of trying to arrest someone in such a setting. But Judas had been here before and knew just where to go. Finally they approached the familiar clearing and were surprised when Jesus stepped forward to meet them. Judas didn't even need to go through with his little charade of affection. But having come this far, he felt he had to follow his course all the way to the end, so he stepped forward and kissed him affectionately (see Matt. 26:49). The traitorous act tore at the tender heart of Jesus, and His pathos is palpable as He laments, "Judas, would you betray the Son of man with a kiss?" (Luke 22:48, RSV). It was a stinging rebuke. If Judas had indeed felt important leading the posse to Jesus, he suddenly felt small and dirty.

As the soldiers stepped forward to seize Jesus, there was a blinding flash that sent them sprawling like dead men (see John 18:6). Their earlier sense of foreboding was well placed. Surely nothing good could come of this foray into the blackness of the night. And what was that blinding flash? Was Judas flattened with the rest? It appears so (verse 5). Yet as he stood up and dusted himself off, he quivered with both fear and excitement; fear that Jesus was starting to exercise His power and that he, Judas, had badly miscalculated and would now lose any role he might have had in the new kingdom. But for that one brief shining moment, he thrilled with the exciting thought that this was just the kind of power play that he had hoped Jesus would perform. Nevertheless, the thought died quickly, for after a brief and clumsy bit of swordplay by Peter, Jesus rebuffed any kind of resistance by His disciples: "Put your sword back into its place. . . . Do you think that I cannot appeal to my Father, and he will at once send me more then twelve legions of angels?" (Matt 26:52, 53, RSV). As they regain their composure and scramble back to their feet, they are amazed to see Him still standing there in the moonlight. He hadn't run away. So they again step forward, though a bit more tentatively than before. When He makes no defensive move, they seize Him and begin leading Him away. Judas is rudely brushed aside, as he is now of absolutely no importance. He now shuffles along, trailing the group he so recently led, mystified and curious to see what will happen next. One thing is clear: his plan is rapidly unraveling.

But he must have asked himself these obvious and reasonable questions: What was Jesus' purpose in this display of His power? Why the flash with no follow-through? Did He do it simply for its "wow" effect? If so, it was the only such event in His entire life. Never had He made a display of power only for effect. Every event He had orchestrated had been driven by some important caring or redemptive purpose. Perhaps His display of power was one last attempt to appeal to their sense of caution; one last attempt to bring them to their senses; one final appeal to Judas to throw himself down at Jesus' feet and confess Him as Lord and acknowledge that His lordship was based not on His power, but on His surrender of His power. It was a dramatic statement of the kind of power He was surrendering—a hint that He would never use His power to coerce or overwhelm the many weaknesses of humans.

Judas' mind is again terribly muddled. Things have gone terribly wrong. As he stumbles along he isn't sure what has become of the 11; he knows only that he wants to keep out of their sight. The various statements Jesus had made about betrayal, so cryptic and opaque to the 11, were now transparent, and he didn't want to have to explain. He drifted along with the crowd to the house of Caiaphas and watched helplessly as the "trial" proceeded. He was familiar with Jewish law and knew that it was illegal to arrest a person and start a trial on the same day. It was one of many safeguards the Jews had written into their laws to help them guard against trying and punishing the innocent. Judas was appalled to see them blithely brush aside any encumbrance to their intended goal—the condemnation of Jesus.

Judas couldn't stand it. It is one thing to have serious disagreements with a person; it is quite another to see that person abused, even tortured, because of your disagreement. Borne down by guilt and remorse, he turned away from scenes that revolted him. In a daze of conflicting thoughts he began wandering aimlessly. As he wandered, he reflected on all that had happened in recent months. He had never wanted to become an enemy of Jesus. In fact, he was very much attracted to Jesus. "He loved the Great Teacher, and desired to be with Him. He felt a desire to be changed in character and life, and he hoped to experience this through connecting himself with Jesus" (*The Desire of Ages,* p. 717). But Judas had come to Jesus the way we so often do—for minor adjustments. Jesus, however, is never satisfied to fix a little symptom here and there. His goal for His followers is transformation and redemption, not correction of a few flaws. Of course, this requires surrender of the life, not surrender of four bad habits.

Knowing Judas' increasing reservations, Jesus had been extremely patient with him. When He had sent out the disciples on their missionary journeys, He had sent Judas along with the others, and even endowed him "with power to heal the sick and the cast out devils. But Judas did not come up to the point of surrendering himself fully to Christ. He did not give up his worldly ambition or his love of money" *(ibid.,* p. 717). Thus Judas was another of the many examples of the infinite patience and condescension of Heaven's Hound. He not only tracks down wandering children, but even uses them in various ways while they are still wandering. We so often suggest that we must achieve a certain level of sainthood before God will use us to do His work and tell His story. But the account of Judas denies that idea. Jesus allowed him to be a channel of divine power even though he had not surrendered, nor would he ever fully surrender, his heart. While it is not a fact to flaunt, it is a thought that comforts. Jesus doesn't keep us at arm's length until we clean up. He meets us wherever we are and, right there, starts whatever process He knows will have a redemptive, though not coercive, influence on us. And as mentioned above, that may even include speaking through us to others even before all the dross has been skimmed off our lives.

Judas suddenly realized it was dawn and found himself back near the scene of the trial. As he walked, the sound of the money jangling in his leather pouch rankled on his nerves. For some unexplained reason, that foolish pouch felt like a boil on his belt. It's all he can feel, it's all he can now think about. His conscience, his guilt, his sense of condemnation, a sense of judgment to come—all bear down on him. He elbows his way through the crowd right into the midst of the proceedings and easily gets the attention of the authorities. He explains that he has made a terrible mistake and that they must let Jesus go. He even promises to return the money. But it is not to be that easy. Caiaphas roughly repulses Judas and tells him they haven't time for his guilt-ridden interruption. His anxiety and self-recrimination are his problem. "But you don't understand! The man may be a hoax, but at worst He is a harmless hoax. He certainly hasn't done anything worthy of death. I have betrayed an innocent man!"

"And what is that to us? Don't try to tell us that your problem is somehow our problem. Now please leave, and let us continue with our business."

Suddenly his cherished money pouch feels as though it weighs a ton. He had loved that money pouch and the influence and power that seemed to come with it. That which had earlier meant so much to him he now despises. His "success" has turned to ashes in his mouth. In a paroxysm of fear and guilt he tears the pouch from his belt, flings it clattering to the floor, and bolts through the crowd and out into the street. The hour that followed was the most awesome of his life, for in it he decided his eternal fate. Heaven's Hound has found him again, but cannot save him against his will. Even now it is not too late, but the choice is his to make. Given his messianic presuppositions, he must have been the kind of Jew who spent time with the holy writings and perhaps had even recited that wonderful promise of forgiveness, "If my people . . . humble themselves, and pray and seek my face, and turn from their wicked ways, then I will hear from heaven, and will forgive their sin" (2 Chron. 7:14, RSV). Judas' wicked way is still forgivable, but he must humble himself, own up to his terrible mistakes and pride, and accept mercy and forgiveness from the Man he has just betrayed. He should have been able to do that. He had heard Jesus many times. He had walked with Him day after day. He had seen the love in His eyes for those who had given up all hope; he had witnessed repeated illustrations of His great forgiving love. But even if he would be granted forgiveness for his treachery, there was no question that he would lose considerable face over his role this night. No, the price was too high. He would find a rope instead. That rope would turn out to be a permanent solution to what could have been a temporary problem.

As Judas, rope in hand, makes his way toward the city gate, he happens upon a familiar and forlorn figure of a man dragging his feet and shuffling toward the same exit from the city. Judas picks up his pace enough to catch up and suddenly recognizes the profile of a pathetic Peter. Judas keeps to the shadows lest he be recognized and have to engage in conversation. He watches as Peter turns down the path that leads through the Kidron and over toward Gethsemane from whence he had come just a few hours before. Judas watches until Peter turns another corner and disappears. Judas takes a different path that runs alongside a ravine. Two men, two betrayals, two paths, two decisions—one led to bitter weeping (Luke 22:62), repentance, and life. The other led to remorse, recrimination, and death. Matthew gives the terse conclusion: "He went and hanged himself" (Matt. 27:5, RSV). Dr. Luke paints a more visceral scene by stating that "falling headlong, he burst asunder in the midst and all his bowels gushed out" (Acts 1:18). Perhaps he selected a poor limb for his rope noose, which snapped when he leaped, resulting in the fatal fall.

It was a pathetic end to a life of great promise. And it is even more pathetic if it doesn't lead us to the question: What am I to learn from this tragedy? First, it is important that we are not too hard on Judas and too easy on ourselves. Passing critical judgment on another is usually only a preliminary to exonerating and enhancing our own self-image. The contrast between us and Judas may not be as great as we might like to think. He was not a born loser or a natural hater. He did not come on the scene as a sneering skeptic. He came to listen, to learn, and to be convinced. He came to have his curiosity satisfied and, once satisfied, to enlist and march into war as a soldier in the new Messiah's army. But like vast numbers of Christian soldiers, Judas' concept had the battle end in victory, whereas Jesus' concept ended in surrender. It was not a new concept for Judas, but it was one he never liked. He had seen and heard Jesus so frequently that he understood the meaning when Jesus said that anyone who would become His disciple must be willing to "deny himself, and take up his cross, and follow me" (Matt. 16:24). But self-denial, never popular, was especially onerous to Judas. He wanted to believe Jesus was special and powerful and messianic, but His continuous theme of self-denial and surrender simply didn't square with Judas' preconception of Jesus' role and mission. He could never quite accept the notion that surrender is the path to success. He was not always traitorous. In fact, he started where we all start—away from God, but willing to listen. His fall into darkness was not sudden; it came in increments, and that is a vital lesson in this story. The light of day and the light of soul both sink ever so gradually. It is a lesson of caution, not for the hardened skeptic, but for all who consider themselves modern-day disciples. But a daily acknowledgment of and surrender to His lordship will ensure that our light will not gradually die out, but rather will continue to increase in brilliance until it one day shines all over the neighborhood, all over our church, and all over the world.

CHAPTER 12

NICODEMUS:
"Other Sheep I Have . . ."

EVEN A HOUND CAN HAVE A DELICATE TOUCH, as when a wet nose nudges the back of your hand, teasing for a snack. Heaven's Hound, as we have seen, takes many tacks, but always well tailored to the needs and makeup of the person approached. When Nicodemus comes into focus in John 3, we see again this tailored, personalized approach of the heavenly Tracker. Nicodemus needed some nudging, but not a blow to the head, like Jonah or Samson. After all, he was not off in some wild wilderness of worldly womanizing. He was not a rebel. In fact, he was a stalwart in a prominent community of believers. Jesus called him "the teacher of Israel" (John 3:10, NASB). The definite article was intentional and instructive. It "points to his pre-eminence as a teacher, and therefore as one who should have known the truth about God and his people" (Howard Clarke Kee, "Nicodemus," *The Interpreter's Dictionary of the Bible* [Nashville: Abingdon Press, 1962], vol. 3, p. 547). For years he had lived and studied in the secure setting of fellow Jews and scholars. He was rich. "The Talmud says of him that he could have fed the entire population of Israel for ten days—very rich and highly esteemed" (Daniel-Rops, *Jesus and His Times* [New York: E. P. Dutton & Co., 1956], p. 153). He was "a ruler of the Jews," usually interpreted to mean he was a member of the Sanhedrin, the highest ruling body of the Jews. His word was valued, his judgment mature, and his theological ideas orthodox. When questions arose, people had learned to turn to Nicodemus for the really solid and safe answers. His profile fits the word *famous,* but hardly the word *fugitive.* All was not as it seemed, however.

Of late, the questions had become much more troublesome as they frequently focused on the mysterious young Rabbi-come-lately, Jesus from Nazareth. He seemed to pose a very large distraction from what was really important to Nicodemus. Just as Catholics are known for their celebrating of Mass, and Adventists are known for their stress on the Saturday Sabbath and the Second Coming, Nicodemus and his fellow Pharisees were renowned for their thorough knowledge of and practice of the law. Furthermore, a vital part of their belief system was the conviction that when the Messiah appeared, He would be a perfect interpreter of the law and would spend His time leading the entire nation into a deeper understanding of the law. Of course, they also believed that He would totally humiliate the Romans—perhaps by a series of powerful miracles that would elevate the Jewish nation to a pinnacle of power and prestige that would be the envy of every nation on earth.

That very preoccupation with miracles set the stage for the beginning of the Nicodemus story. In John 2:11 the result of Jesus' water-to-wine miracle was that "his disciples believed on him." That incident is immediately followed in the Gospel of John by Jesus' first Temple cleansing, after which His opponents issue the demand for a sign before they will believe (verse 18). Then verse 23 puts Jesus at the Passover feast in Jerusalem, where "many believed in his name when they saw the signs which he did" (RSV). But Jesus knew the shallow nature of faith based on signs (John consistently uses the word *signs* for miracles); hence, the comment in verses 24, 25: "But Jesus did not trust himself to them, because he knew . . . what was in man" (RSV). In other words, He knew that faith that needs miracles to prop it up is not the unshakable faith that moves people to trust Him when nothing good is happening, let alone when no miracles are present. The very next verse (John 3:1) is the beginning of the Nicodemus story. Given the preoccupation with signs (miracles) and belief in those preceding verses, it is quite clear that John is preparing the reader for the real Nicodemus question: "What is it with this Miracle Worker?"

The Pharisees were the party of teachers among the Jews, and they needed acceptance and influence with the crowds if they were to be effective. Consequently when a new voice that attracted a significant following arose, they made it a practice to check it out. It could represent competition. Accordingly, they had sent a delegation over to the Jordan, traveling that treacherous trail to check out the desert recluse known as John the Baptizer. Given the terrain and the legendary danger along that road, it was not an easy trip from Jerusalem to Jordan and back, so it indicates the depth of their curiosity to check out what they considered competitive influences. Nicodemus had gone with the group, but the strange preaching and style of John had left him unconvinced and unconvicted (*The Desire of Ages,* p. 171). You could say that the first invitations of the voice of conscience were rebuffed. But the Hound of Heaven is at once infinitely patient and ever relentless.

Time had passed, and Nicodemus had heard that this Jesus, who did not claim to be a rabbi, acted like one by traveling about, teaching a small group of learners (the actual meaning of the term *disciple* is "one who learns"). That whole scenario raised two very large questions in the mind of Nicodemus. First, though Jesus acted and sounded like a rabbi, no one remembered Him going through any of the well-known rabbinical training. And second, what was he to make of all the miracle stories? Nicodemus had lost count of the number of times he had been asked about the source of Jesus' training. "Where did he go to synagogue school?" "What kind of degree does he have?" "Why don't we remember him going through synagogue training?" To each such question Nicodemus could answer only "I don't know." But lately the questions had gotten more specific. "Rabbi, what do you think about what Jesus said about divorce?" "Rabbi, have you heard what Jesus said in Cana the other day?" "No, I haven't heard. What did he say?" And so it went. But it was when people asked, "But why is he so popular?" that Nicodemus and his friends did their slow burn. Human egos nearly always take punishing blows when someone with less qualification gets all the recognition. Their response to all the Jesus interest was usually something like "It isn't important what Jesus said, only what the law says." But to some that was sounding increasingly like a sidestep, with a pinch of pettiness thrown in. Nicodemus had heard it and had said it, but he no longer felt good about saying it. The fact is, the Jesus questions had become a fixation, and fixations can sometimes take us by the throat and threaten to squeeze out our very breath until we have dealt with them.

Then word came that Jesus was coming to Jerusalem, and

Nicodemus was delighted to hear the rumor—though with his friends he maintained a stoic calm about the news, feigning lack of interest so as to protect his reputation. After all, he was the teacher of Israel. The teacher of Israel shouldn't need another teacher teaching him what to teach. But neither he nor his friends understood the relentless nature of the nudging of the Hound of Heaven. On the fateful day of their first encounter Nicodemus was completely flummoxed by what he witnessed. He had expected Jesus to sit down in some prominent place and teach His disciples, while a small crowd stood and sat around listening in. Nicodemus could then stand at the back or around a corner and listen for himself. Instead Jesus came directly to the Temple and created a scene of violence and pandemonium. After a couple of cutting remarks to the leading Sadducees, Jesus grabbed a rope and with it started a small stampede, driving out the animals from the Temple area and, in the process, making sure the cash tables got knocked over. It was a noisy and confusing melee.

Nicodemus was incredulous. His shock arose not from complete disapproval, but simply that the young, noncredentialed teacher had had the nerve to rebuke the esteemed Sadducees. They were the party of the priesthood, and the Temple activities were largely under their direction. But there was little love lost between them and the party of teachers that made up the Pharisees. In fact, the tension between the two groups was such that Nicodemus, proud Pharisee that he was, may have actually felt a certain satisfied smugness that the Sadducees had been publicly humiliated. At the same time, he knew how all the leaders would react to this humiliating event. He knew that with that bold stroke the inexperienced, untrained young Rabbi had set the stage for a deadly feud. Jesus would now be blacklisted. If Nicodemus was ever to interview Him, his close friends and the many who had viewed Him as their teacher could never know of the interview.

It was days before the shock wave and reverberations of the Temple cleansing simmered down. Even then the prime topic of many discussions, especially among the theologians, was the impact of that event. "What was his real reason for doing it?" "What do you think he meant by 'my Father's house'?" "Why couldn't he leave well enough alone? The whole operation was bringing in an additional 500 shekels a month and 3,000 shekels the month of the Passover." "Well, you know what they say: 'There are only two kinds of people in the world—those who like to ride in the boat and those who like to rock the boat.' This Jesus is definitely one of the latter."

But on that shocking day after Jesus had cleared out the herd and the rabble, Nicodemus had stood discreetly out of sight and had watched and listened as Jesus then received the poor, healed the sick, and taught the people who had the courage to trickle back into the Temple. What he heard were hardly the words of an insurrectionist or of a lawbreaking radical. They were the words of a gentle, self-assured Scholar who spoke without hesitation, and whose authority seemed to be His own. He didn't quote even one of the renowned rabbis to give His words credence—a common teaching technique of the time.

A wind of restlessness was blowing across the inner soul of Nicodemus. To return to our metaphor, Heaven's Hound was closing in on him. It was as if a wet nose were nudging him in a direction he couldn't yet perceive or understand. All he knew was that he felt a growing desire to hear Jesus close up, to examine Him himself, to ask Him some of the same questions that people had so often put to Him. "Where were you trained?" "Why do the crowds follow you so avidly?" "And those miracles—how do you do them, and is there some deeper meaning we should attach to them?" The questions just kept hanging there. For a time he tried to dismiss them, but to no avail.

But there was something else he couldn't dismiss: the pressure of his skeptical friends. And such pressure knows no boundaries of time or place. For good or ill, we are all confronted and, in varying degrees, shaped by such pressure. As we mature we are often counseled to "have a mind of your own." But from youth to old age our minds and attitudes are being molded by external influences. We all live and move about in a cultural time and place that bombards us with a dizzying array of suggestions and pressures—pressures that span the spectrum from the sublime to the ridiculous, from the sincere to the cynical, from nurturing to nay-saying. Pressures to conform or to rebel never really go away. They can cause Samson to marry a Philistine or a current Christian to wear a nose stud. To sort out the divine from the devilish unerringly is simply not humanly possible. Left to himself, Nicodemus could not have made sense of the competing voices that simultaneously urged him to go to Jesus and to stay away from Jesus. But above, behind, and through all the noisy and conflicting influences comes the soft padding of those "strong Feet that followed, followed after." That Heavenly Hound does not lose us or forget us or abandon us to the din that constantly surrounds us. The restless stirring in the heart of Nicodemus was evidence once again that "a Voice beat more instant than the Feet," and it was that voice that gradually silenced the suggestions of the skeptics about Jesus. Nicodemus had to seek Him out. Needless to say, the consequences to Nicodemus of following that inner voice were daunting—they usually are. Weighty decisions are often accompanied with high price tags. Any hint of serious interest in Jesus would surely alienate many, if not most, of his colleagues and close friends. Would he lose his position in the Sanhedrin? Would he be ostracized, even banned, from the synagogue in which he loved to teach?

But the consequences of not listening to that voice were even more daunting. The voice would continue to nag him. And if Jesus was indeed the One who was to come, what if he, "the teacher of Israel," turned away from Him? No, he dare not look the other way; he had to investigate. The miracle stories demanded it. But having seen the intractable, even ruthless manner of his fellow Sanhedrins with dissenters, it was only prudent to keep his curiosity quiet. Was it timidity or discretion that lay behind his coming at night? Or did nighttime simply ensure an uninterrupted and more leisurely interview? After all, Jesus' days were often filled with activity and with crowds of people, and Nicodemus wanted Jesus' undivided attention. Only on a quiet evening could he be assured of that. The important point is that he put aside all misgivings and followed up on the promptings of that inner voice. He somehow made the arrangements and went.

Given all the preoccupation with signs/miracles (John 2:11, 18, 22, 23), it is not surprising that Nicodemus' opening statement reveals his belief that miracles provide impeccable evidence that a person is very tight with God, "for no one can do these signs . . .unless God is with him" (John 3:2, RSV). On the surface it sounds like a simple statement of fact. But Nicodemus didn't seek out Jesus in the dark of night simply to state what many believed was obvious. No, tucked away in that statement were some well-concealed questions. Nicodemus was clearly enamored of Jesus' miracles. In a very real sense they had brought him to Jesus. But they had brought him because he didn't really understand how they worked or what they meant. And, of course, behind the mystery of the miracles was the meaning of the Man. Nicodemus didn't quite know what to make of Him, and he wanted to know without people knowing that he wanted to know. But he was either too proud or else really didn't know how to frame the questions that had been nagging all his quiet, thoughtful hours. So although he started with a statement, he was really fishing for answers to very pressing concerns. Fortunate for Nicodemus, Jesus knew everything there was to know about "fishing" expeditions. So Jesus went straight to the hidden questions and brought them out for all to see. "It's not about miracles or even about Me; it's about you, Nicodemus." And that statement harks back to John 2:25: "For he knew what was in man."

That is at once scary and reassuring. Scary in that every honest human has hidden away a few embarrassments, a few (or many) private moments of selfish pride or worse that they hope no one will ever know. We might call it the Nicodemus syndrome. Always keep the discussions intellectual and impersonal and remember that privacy is one of our most basic human rights. Yet here we are reminded that He knows our inner thoughts, that we have no secrecy, no privacy, from God. Behind all our closed doors He is always looking over our shoulders. Scary! But at the same time that thought is wonderfully reassuring when we remember how He uses all that information about our private lives. He is much like the parent of a 3-year-old. No one worries much that a 3-year-old has no privacy from parents. The normal assumption is that the one goal of such a parent is the protection and care of the child, and all knowledge is used to that end. So it is with God. He knows all there is to know about us, but uses that knowledge for one goal—our redemption. Scary? No. Reassuring? Absolutely.

It was because He knew what was "in" Nicodemus that Jesus didn't bother to answer his question about miracles and the source of His power. Instead He went straight to the heart of the matter. Jesus knew that the reason Heaven's Hound approaches wandering humans in a dizzying array of disguises is that they have so many elaborate ways of hiding from Him. In other words, no matter what shape their masquerade takes, He can outmasquerade them. By his attempting to quiz Jesus about the source of His power and miracles, Nicodemus was continuing to evade the implications of the voice of conscience and the urgings of the Spirit. He had come, physically, to Jesus, but he was still making a valiant effort to hide behind his moral rectitude. Jesus deftly stepped into his hiding place and said, "Boo!"

Actually, it came out in that abrupt statement about a rebirth: "Very truly, I tell you, no one can see the kingdom of God without being born from above" (John 3:3, NRSV). Nicodemus reacted about the same as if someone really had said "Boo!" The erudite Pharisee was surprised and flustered by the thought that he was in any sense "unborn." The elderly, respected scholar was used to people making a bit of a fuss over him. But the young Rabbi, while polite and gentle, showed no particular deference. He didn't seem terribly excited over the prospect of making a convert out of an old and respected member of the Sanhedrin. Nicodemus' demeanor, on the other hand, seemed to include an element of condescension. He purported to be speaking for a group as he began by saying, "We know you are a godly teacher, because an impostor couldn't perform all those wonder works." In other words, he seemed to be saying, "Several of us have been discussing your case and have concluded that you are not a fraud, since frauds can't do miracles." Obviously Nicodemus and whoever he was including in the "we" were completely taken by the miracles.

But Jesus didn't thank Nicodemus for the faint compliment, nor pause to fawn over the nice statement. Nor does He take the time to try to correct the flawed reasoning that led Nicodemus and his friends to their shallow conclusion about the value of miracles. Instead Jesus began at the same level as Nicodemus, almost as though they were two equals—two teachers discussing theological matters. Except that Jesus quickly merged the personal with the theological, since that was where Nicodemus needed the most help. "It is well and good that you have not dismissed Me as a fraud, but merely to seize upon My miracles as the indication that I am not a fraud is not enough. A cool decision of the mind will bring you only partway, Nicodemus. Something deeper, mysterious, experiential, must be included. To truly perceive the meaning of My life and teachings requires something more radical, like a second birth experience—only this one is 'from above.' " (The phrase in John 3:3 is best translated "born from above," rather than the more tepid "born again").

The abrupt shift in the conversation from Jesus' miracles to

Nicodemus' rebirth was hardly welcomed by Nicodemus. Perhaps he had intended to say something further, such as "We believe you have been sent to restore the kingdom to Israel, and I have come to give you some advice on how best to go about it." But Jesus cut him short. "Your ideas of the Messiah and His kingdom are much too narrow. You are bound to earth views, and what you must have is the view from above. The kingdom is not established or entered into by human strength of will and determination. It certainly is not advanced by a more rigorous interpretation and practice of the law. Nor will it be brought about by a new method of evangelism. It is not even helped along by a dash of magic and a miracle here and there.

"It is a new birth that is required; that no care spent on our conduct, no improvement and refinement of the natural man suffices. For flying it is not an improved caterpillar that is needed, it is a butterfly; it is not a caterpillar of finer colour or more rapid movement or larger proportions, it is a new creature" (Marcus Dods, *The Gospel of St. John, The Expositor's Bible* [New York: Hodder and Stoughton, n.d.], vol. 1, p. 115).

As we have seen, conversions come wrapped in a wide variety of colors. The conversion stories I grew up hearing were always such dramatic things. "I was living a life of debauchery, but one night as the music played and the speaker gave his invitation the Spirit spoke to my heart, and I went forward. My life has never been the same since. Praise God!" "I was well into a life of crime. I was in jail for 'grand theft auto.' I had reached the very bottom. But through a series of incredible events, Jesus came into my life. It was miracle after miracle. He turned my life around. Now all I want to do is serve Him." Those were the guest speakers brought in for those special youth meetings, those big affairs when several churches came together and met in a large auditorium. The warnings about the devil and the dark side of our world made deep impressions on our young minds. Except I couldn't remember a time when I hadn't gone to Sabbath school and church. In fact, I was one of those who almost always got a little silver star in Sabbath school because I could say all the memory verses for a whole quarter. The only time I could remember our family missing church was one time on a long vacation trip to California. And even that time we looked for a church, but couldn't find one. As a result we spent the day not traveling, but still feeling vaguely guilty because we weren't in church. Given that kind of upbringing, I often wondered just what all a life of debauchery might include. In spite of the warnings, I often felt I had missed out on something not simply dangerous, but probably exciting and maybe even fun. But more important, I also felt I had missed a vital element in the conversion process. That most important first step—the life of crime and debauchery—was missing in my life. Maybe I wasn't converted at all. Maybe I couldn't be converted until there was something really bad to be converted from.

But as time passed, another thought gradually developed—more insidious than the first. It centered in thankfulness for my goodness; thankfulness for what I wasn't, with just a hint of pride for what I was. I wasn't one of those rebellious, hard-core sinners; I was like the obedient child in all the children's stories who got the larger piece of pie because I had obeyed, even when mother was gone to get groceries. She had said don't play with matches, and I had obeyed. I was well on my way to becoming a young Nicodemus. Those of us who, like Nicodemus, have grown up "good" often live with the illusion that a few minor repairs are all that our lives require. "Surely my faithful church attendance counts for something." It was that kind of thinking that prompted one of Jesus' most telling stories—about two would-be worshippers, one of whom, a Pharisee like Nicodemus, was thankful he was "not like other men, extortioners, unjust, adulterers" (Luke 18:11, RSV). According to Jesus, however, his prayer was only "with himself." But the other man, the one who confessed his sinfulness, "went down to his house justified" (verse 14, RSV). Clearly, being thankful that you are good is not enough. In fact, that attitude is what caused the noun *Pharisee* to become an adjective, *pharisaical,* meaning proud of one's attainments. As we have seen, famous fugitives have chosen a wide variety of hiding places, and Nicodemus shows us that a person can hide behind moral rectitude as readily as one can hide in an immoral swamp. In fact, for large numbers of contemporary Christians, it is more likely that a legalistic religiosity, rather than a life of rebellion, will keep them away from the Lord. It is one of the most important lessons of the Nicodemus story: good people are not necessarily converted people. A life of quiet compliance may have only law at the center of it. And keeping the law a little more faithfully this year than last may include just a smidgen of pride, but that little pinch of pride may be just enough to crowd out the sense of need of a Savior.

Which raises the issue of how conversion of "good" people happens. Clear biblical examples are few. There is, of course, the dramatic Damascus road confrontation, which knocked Saul of Tarsus off his horse and into a changed life (Acts 9:4). And there is the Philippian jailer who, when he was saved from certain death by the honesty of Paul and Silas, fell trembling before them with the plea "What must I do to be saved?" (Acts 16:30)—the most typical conversion question. But as mentioned above, while that kind of drama is the theme of many a modern youth congress sermon, it is not the paradigm for the conversion story of most churchgoing young people. A more pertinent biblical example is that of the disciples, who began their walk with Jesus in a state of considerable naïveté. Very gradually, over a period of years, they came to understand just what a Messiah was all about and what their acceptance of Him would mean for their life choices. Then, near the end of His time with them, "he breathed on them, and said to them, 'Receive the Holy Spirit' " (John 20:22, RSV). If, as Jesus explained to Nicodemus, conversion included being born of water and of the Spirit, then the disciples' conversion stories had both parts, but they were separated by years. Much earlier John had baptized some of them in water for the repentance of their sins. Years later after an extended period of learning from Jesus all about His teachings, He finally is able to "baptize" them with the Holy Spirit, and their conversion is, at last, complete. And so it can happen with modern-day disciples—a genuine conversion must include the aspects of baptism of repentance from sin and baptism of the Spirit for power to live the life. But the complete conversion story can take time, when looked at from the beginning to end. Time during which there is a gradual maturing in the faith. Thunder and lightning may play no role at all. There may be no dramatically visible change from folly to faith, or from cocaine to Christian. Accordingly the conversion of an "upright" person may consist of a gradually developing conviction that a life of law is lost without the Lord. Such a conviction of the mind, though quiet and gradual, is as thorough and attitude-altering as any of the more explosive, sudden scenarios. But a clear, quiet, and gradual surrender just doesn't appear as convincing or as real as the more dramatic variety.

Nicodemus' whole illusion of inherent human goodness was shattered under the hammer blow of Jesus' declaration "You must be born from above if you are to see the kingdom of God" (see John 3:3). While that concept of radical change seemed to genuinely shock Nicodemus, his shock was not in the concept, but in the thought that it was required of Jews. For years Jews had taught that "converts from heathenism to the faith of Israel were . . . compared to children just born" (*The Desire of Ages,* p. 171). But that Jews, sons of Abraham, members of the covenant community, had to be converted and baptized was unthinkable. Furthermore, that he, *the* teacher of Israel, was considered in some sense unconverted was close to scandalous. But, of course, Jesus had developed a reputation for saying scandalous things. It seems clear that Nicodemus' bafflement was not because he misunderstood Jesus' metaphorical terms, but because he understood well the implications and was offended because it would be personally humbling.

In response to Nicodemus' protest "How can a man be born when he is old?" (verse 4), Jesus referred to the wind as an example of both the mystery and power of the Spirit (verse 8). Like his concept of the Messiah and of the coming kingdom, Nicodemus' view of the working of the Spirit was too limiting, too small, because it was quite vague and ill-defined. Our view, on the other hand, is usually too small because it is too prescribed and well-defined. We, along with Nicodemus, must expand our understanding of the Spirit's involvement in our rebirth and in living the life that follows. As mentioned before, heavenly methods simply defy our human prescriptions. Nicodemus gave little thought to a Jewish conversion, let alone any prodding by the Holy Spirit. In some contrast, we acknowledge the conversion process but are prone to tie the Spirit's working to well-known, familiar settings, such as evangelistic appeals accompanied by soft music. But Jesus makes the Spirit's activities more mysterious and at the same time absolutely essential. If in fact His working is as invisible as the wind, we do Him considerable injustice to limit His activities to those we can easily describe.

However, like the wind's, the Spirit's power to change things is beyond question. As the invisible wind can turn a building upside down, the mysterious Spirit can accomplish the seemingly impossible. "Nicodemus, how do you explain your being here this dark hour, when all your instincts kept telling you to stay away? That compulsion that finally drove you, against your fears, to set up this interview—do you, for one minute, think you did that all by yourself? You see,

Nicodemus, every impression that nudges us toward the kingdom is God's doing, not ours. That's what it means to be born of the Spirit." The precise nature of those impressions is unpredictable, inexplicable, and unrelenting. He can and will do whatever is necessary to surround us with an environment that nurtures and develops us, even though at the time His working is as invisible as the wind.

The immediate outcome of the interview is a mystery. In the following verses John imperceptibly moves from the Nicodemus narrative into the issue of God's purpose in sending Christ into the world, which includes, in John 3:16, the clearest and best-known description of God's love. As John continues, Nicodemus simply fades from view. But he reappears in two instructive episodes later in the same Gospel. In John 7:45-52 John describes an abortive attempt to arrest Jesus—which fails because those sent to arrest Him get so caught up in His stories that they can't bring themselves to do it. The chief rabbis are furious, and in the ensuing debate feelings are running high. In that setting the lone voice of Nicodemus speaks out for caution and fairness. He reminds them of their own law in Deuteronomy 19:15, in which they are forbidden to prejudge someone without a careful listening to that person's side of the issue. Even though he very cautiously puts it in the form of a question, he suspects how it will be interpreted—and he is right. In verse 52, with many a barbed look at Nicodemus, they ask, "Are you from Galilee too? Search and you will see that no prophet is to rise from Galilee" (RSV).

It was an especially loaded question for Nicodemus. For many years there had been bitter feelings between the leaders in Jerusalem and those who lived in the northern territory of Galilee. The animosity may have arisen many years before, when the southern nation of Judah was taken into captivity, while many peasants in the northern regions were left to care for the land. When the captivity ended, those who returned from Babylon settled in the south and considered themselves the true people of God. They also held in disdain those northern Jews, some of whom had intermarried with non-Jews and were considered by the Jews of Jerusalem to be renegades and outside the pale of God's concern. So it is not surprising that the leading rabbis considered Galileans reprobates—from whom God would never choose a prophet. In their anger and frustrated state of mind they either forgot about Jonah, who came from Galilee, or else didn't consider him to be a legitimate prophet. Even more striking is this tacit denial that Jesus, who came from the northern city of Nazareth, was a prophet.

In John 19:30-40 is Nicodemus' final scene. The chief rabbis have been successful—although hardly in the way they had planned. They have gotten Jesus executed. They had frantically wished that it would not be at the time of the Passover, because at such a time, with lots of visitors, including many Galileans in town, they feared a tumult would result. But the timing was taken out of their hands, as the Lord wanted maximum exposure of the greatest event in human history.

As those cataclysmic events unfolded it was a bold Nicodemus who, along with Joseph of Arimathea, went out to that desecrated hill between the hours of 3:00 p.m. and sundown and became defiled by personally handling the dead body of One who was considered a criminal. With their own hands these two influential men were willing to sacrifice it all—their prestige with colleagues, their reputation in the community, their position, their money—by showing interest in and love for that battered body. With their own hands they managed to get it down off the cross before sundown and convey it to a nearby garden, apparently Joseph's garden, and to lay it in a tomb that Joseph had made ready for his own burial.

By this open act of reverence, Nicodemus made public profession of his being a follower of Christ. His considerable wealth enabled him to provide a huge amount of spices of myrrh and aloes to be placed between the folds of the linen cloth in which they wrapped the body of Jesus. Nicodemus the Pharisee, the one-time fugitive who had hidden for years behind a reputation of perfect lawkeeping, has now become fully and openly just another child of grace. Heaven's Tracker has brought another lost child home.

CHAPTER 13

PAUL:
A Harness for the Headstrong

THERE WAS SOMETHING ABOUT THE GROUP of travelers that just didn't look right. It wasn't simply that the central figure was a blind man. Eye disease and blindness were common ailments of the time. But blind men didn't normally travel with an entourage. In fact, blindness, like so many maladies of the time, was considered something of a curse, so blind people were usually shunned and had mostly to fend for themselves. And blind men were never dressed as well as this blind man. As the group shuffled its way through the city gate and on down the dusty street, it seemed to some of the onlookers that the blind man was considerably less sure on his feet than most blind men—as if his blindness were a recent development. Perhaps some of the bystanders wondered aloud how soon this new unfortunate would be confronting them on their street corners, joining the tattered and unwashed beggars in their constant plea for alms—though at this moment he certainly looked as though he was in no need of alms. Still others may have noticed an attitude of unusual chagrin and an apparent desire to escape from the stare of onlookers as quickly as possible. Whoever these visitors were, their entrance into the city was less than auspicious. Luke puts it this way in Acts 9:8: "They led him by the hand and brought him into Damascus" (RSV). Saul, the brilliant young Pharisee; Saul, the intrepid inquisitor; Saul, the merciless persecutor, had reached his destination. But it wasn't quite the entry he had anticipated. He had taken quite a fall and was in the process of losing a lot more than his eyesight. As few men, Saul was the complete man for his mission. Everything about his background and training lent itself, at this stage in his life, to a feeling of confidence and self-assurance. First, he was Roman by birth and citizenship, and he spoke of it with pride. It served as his passport to distant lands and a defense against mistreatment. When faced with an unjust beating, he could ask, "Is it lawful for you to scourge a man who is a Roman citizen and uncondemned?" (Acts 22:25, RSV). Whereupon the centurion cautioned his commander, "Take care what you do, for this man is a Roman" (see verse 26). Immediately the beating was called off, and the commander was even fearful "after he found out that he was a Roman . . . because he had bound him" (see verse 29). You just don't shackle and beat a Roman citizen without overwhelming evidence of criminal intent. As a citizen of Rome, Saul stood above the common herd. In almost any provincial town he ranked with the aristocracy.

In addition, he was from Tarsus, a university city where an atmosphere of learning was pervasive. Strabo indicates that the city was known for its philosophers, poets, grammarians, and physicians. By culture, environment, and language, Saul was surrounded by Greek influences. The Greek traits of adaptability, curiosity, alertness, and the love of investigation became part of his early molding.

Finally, he was by training a Pharisee and equally proud of that. Furthermore, he was not just another Pharisee, but one of considerable stature. Not all the promising young Jews were privileged to sit at the feet of Gamaliel, considered by many to be the greatest rabbi of all. Perhaps, some even allowed, one day Saul would sit in the august seat of Gamaliel and continue his distinguished traditions. Saul's keen mind and insightful comments had won for him a coveted place in the inner circle of the rabbis. His youthful enthusiasm, coupled with his conservative theology, also stood him in good stead with the leading Pharisees. He would later testify that he had advanced in Judaism beyond many of his contemporaries in his own nation, "being more exceedingly zealous of the traditions of my fathers" (Gal. 1:14).

To say that Saul was well qualified to be a traveling ambassador is a considerable understatement. And now he was about to begin his career in earnest, which for young Pharisees happened when they turned 30. New in his work, he felt he had most of the answers to the troubling questions of life. Self-confidence and the feeling of having all the answers tend to peak early in our careers. But youthful enthusiasm and self-assurance were not the only forces driving Saul. "I . . . was convinced that I ought to do many things in opposing the name of Jesus of Nazareth. . . . I not only shut up many of the saints in prison . . . , but when they were put to death I cast my vote against them. And I punished them often in all the synagogues and tried to make them blaspheme; and in raging fury against them, I persecuted them even to foreign cities" (Acts 26:9-11, RSV). But his frenetic activity was spurred on by another motive—fear that he could be wrong. In the hidden recesses of his conscience lay some nagging doubts about the rightness of his cause. However, we humans have a great tendency to keep our doubts well hidden, and often resort to frantic activity as the best cover. Heaven's Hound was baying in the distance, and Saul tried desperately to quiet the sound by running faster and working harder every day.

So Saul, with his armor all in place, went out conquering and to conquer. But even a suit of armor has its cracks, and they needn't be very large to admit a shaft of light. And that first shaft of light to penetrate his armor shone from the face of Stephen as he fell dying before the eyes of Saul. Sometime in those last moments, as his lifeblood began to stain the dust beneath him, Stephen had expressed that sentiment first enunciated by Jesus: "Lord, do not hold this sin against them" (Acts 7:60, RSV). And Luke, the master storyteller, made this passing comment: "And the witnesses laid down their garments at the feet of a young man named Saul" (verse 58, RSV). Immediately Luke moves on to other stories. However, his seemingly offhand, casual reference to "a young man named Saul" gives the reader the sensation that the spotlight will soon return and illuminate once and for all the precise outline of that face and the person behind it. Or to return to our familiar metaphor, the hearing is rarely so deaf that we can completely muffle the baying of the Hound of Heaven. And for Saul the cries of Stephen as the stones fell were the first faint calls from that heavenly Tracker.

That murder scene and Stephen's sentiment of forgiveness wreaked havoc with some of Saul's presuppositions. The death of that innocent man, a man thoroughly imbued with the forgiving spirit of his Master, made an indelible impression. Years later, when Paul was giving his own defense before a crowd clamoring for his blood, the memory of Stephen's murder rose up before him. In Acts 22:20, as the rabble was about to lose all control, Paul, with pathos oozing from every syllable, lamented: "And when the blood of Stephen thy witness was shed, I also was standing by and approving, and keeping the garments of those who killed him" (RSV).

No doubt the reason that painful memory was so readily available was that it was never far below the level of his conscious mind. The slightest similarity of circumstances or the slightest warmth of conscience breathed life into that skeleton in his closet, and it rose up to hauntingly remind him of the utter wretchedness of those who steel themselves against the voice of conscience and the impressions of the Spirit. The self-sufficient Saul, the well-trained, well-educated Saul, the zealous, indefatigable Pharisee, was no match for the example of the Christ-possessed Stephen. The calm example of the dying Stephen caused Saul some serious misgivings about the rightness of his cause against the followers of Jesus, but he was not yet ready to acknowledge that he could be so wrong. So he once again rebelled "against the voice of conscience and the grace of God" (Ellen G. White, *The Acts of the Apostles,* p. 113).

But even as his rebellion congealed and drove him madly toward violent confrontations in Damascus, another light, not subtle as before, enveloped him, awed him, floored him. "A light from heaven flashed about him. And he fell to the ground" (Acts 9:3, 4, RSV). The irony was that this light brought him total darkness. "When his eyes were opened, he could see nothing; so they led him by the hand" (verse 8, RSV). Jesus had spoken of those who had eyes, yet were blinded by hardened hearts (Mark 8:18). On his way to Damascus, Saul fit that category perfectly. He epitomized the bromide "There are none so blind as those who will not see." But God, who is infinitely patient, saw the potential of this talented man and knew that a plunge into darkness was the only path that would successfully lead him to see the light.

That point has endless applications. When the darkness of pain, of a broken relationship, of uncertainty, of grief, descends upon us, how rarely are we able to see even a small glimmer of light. In fact, the darkness often deepens under a blanket of whys or of noisy accusations about the unfairness of life and of the God who is supposed to protect His children from hurts and suffering. But the fact that Saul's blackout was the necessary prelude to his spiritual sunrise should teach us patience and trust for those dark hours that sooner or later descend upon every earthbound human.

In the darkness of his Damascus room Saul had time for serious reflection. For three days this eminent fellow with the expense account, whose trip was funded by the brethren in Jerusalem—this fellow who had come to town with a coterie of servants at his beck and call—sat in darkness, entertaining no visitors, searching desperately for answers. But if God had a message for him, why the blindness? He could have been made lame like Jacob. He could have been struck dumb like Zacharias. But blindness? Saul knew of the stigma that was attached to blindness. It was still looked upon as a consequence of sin. In fact, it is included in a list of physical disabilities (Lev. 21:20) that disqualified a man from the priesthood—and it could be either congenital or acquired. Clearly it was particularly embarrassing and humiliating to a prominent young Pharisee. Was that the reason it was chosen? Or was it because one of the prime functions of the ministry of Jesus was the "recovering of sight to the blind" (Luke 4:18)? Was Saul to be the embodiment and summary of the ministry of Jesus?

We often wonder about the suddenness of Saul's conversion, the seeming overwhelming power of God and the implications for Saul's freedom of choice. Most conversions don't start with a frightening fall to the ground, brought on by something equivalent to a blow to the head. But the suddenness may have been more apparent than real. It was not accidental that Luke, much earlier, juxtaposed the dying testimony of Stephen ("Lord, do not hold this sin against them" [Acts 7:60, RSV]) with the introduction of Saul. In other words, by the time Luke wrote that story he was well aware of what a piercing moment for Saul the death of Stephen was. Luke had come to sense that that event had planted a seed of doubt in Saul's mind, which took many days to germinate. Then, too, the Damascus road experience was followed by three days of darkness spent in silent contemplation of all these recent events. This entire time, then, must figure prominently in the total conversion experience, for conversion involves much more than a sudden impulse. A bolt of lightning and a thunderclap have yet to produce a Christian. Even a talking donkey and an angel from heaven aren't enough to bring conversion—as the story of Balaam clearly indicates (Num. 22-24). Such special effects are obviously part of God's arsenal to arrest our attention, but grace and all it means takes hold of us only after we have had time to think and reflect meaningfully on whatever confrontation God's Spirit has put before us. Consequently, it is incorrect to speak of Saul's conversion on the Damascus road. There God dramatically confronted him, but it was only after days of quiet reflection that he was able to sort it all out and surrender his will completely to God's direction. Thus his conversion, though bombastic at the start, seems to conclude with a subdued and quiet dialogue with Ananias (Acts 9:17-19). For certain contemporary Christians it should be instructive that no spectacular display of power, such as tongue speech (Acts 2:11; 10:46; 19:6), came to attest to onlookers that Saul's conversion experience was genuine. Of course, the falling "scales" and the return of his eyesight helped convince such skeptics as Ananias ("Lord, I have heard . . . how much evil he has done to thy saints" [Acts 9:13, RSV]) that Saul's conversion was orchestrated from above (as are all conversions, no matter what other events attend them).

It is reasonable that Saul's conversion should be described in such minute detail, for it instructs us in a number of ways. First, he is the only New Testament figure about whom such a dramatic about-face is recorded. Large numbers of people had already come to "believe," but no details are given that spell out any soul-stirring contrast between their "before" and "after" lives. Also, all the other apostles had come to experience faith and trust in Christ as a result of a gradual dawning of the light as they associated with Him and with one another. But the preconverted Saul and the converted Saul are truly different persons. Perhaps God wanted to show future generations of Christians how the preeminent New Testament theologian was dramatically humbled and how, in a relatively short time, he could be changed from persecuting Pharisee to champion believer. If an enemy as implacable as Saul could come to faith and be forgiven and used by God, then surely John Doe Skeptic could also be changed.

Saul's conversion story also helps illustrate how varied are the ways by which human lives can be drawn Godward. David laments, "I was brought forth in iniquity, and in sin did my mother conceive me" (Ps. 51:5, RSV), and if, as he earlier stated, that corrupt beginning includes all of us ("They are all alike corrupt, there is none that does good, no, not one" [Ps. 14:3, RSV]), then every human who is converted must be guided through that experience with "outside" help. We all begin life with our feet planted firmly in the soil of this world and our faces turned away from God. To break that earthly connection and turn our faces toward God requires more than human power. But how that power is manifested we can never predict or systematize. For some it is enough for Heaven's Hound to make Himself known with some quiet music and a gentle invitation. For others He appears in the collective and gradual influences of godly parents, teachers, friends, or siblings. For still others, like Saul, it is almost as if the Tracker has to do more than send up a little howl when He finds us. For the really hard cases it is almost as if He has to sink His teeth into our soft flesh before we will finally say, "OK, OK, I'm listening." To put it a little less dramatically, He is clearly not averse to using a light-and-sound show, if that's what it takes to get our attention. Accordingly, as we have seen and said repeatedly, the redemptive approaches heaven takes are quite impressive in their diversity. Saul's shock wave resulted in a radical transformation of the man, yet his change was not more genuine or more thorough than the gradual and quiet enlightenment of James or John or Peter. This truth should bring a certain solace to generations of Christians who have come to accept the Lord as Savior, yet find no exact parallel between their experience and that recorded in Scripture or in other Christian writings. When the sensational "gangs to God" conversions or even the Pharisee to missionary transformations get too much attention, they can raise questions about the genuineness of the gradual, quiet enlightenment of the mind that cannot be precisely dated. But when Saul's experience is coupled with that of the other apostles, we can know that whether sudden or gradual, whether spectacular or quiet, the conversion phenomenon is real, it is powerful, and it changes the life. God's ways are truly mysterious; they cannot be predicted, quantified, or anticipated.

Saul's "conversion" differed remarkably from what that word has come to mean to Christians. So often that experience is thought of as changing an irreligious person to a religious one, but that conventional understanding hardly fits the apostle. Prior to his "conversion" he could say that "as to righteousness under the law [I was] blameless" (Phil. 3:6, RSV). If conversion is viewed as that which changes a person from licentiousness and immorality to purity and morality, then we have to think in new categories to understand the experience of Saul. In some respects his conversion was similar to the change from one denomination to another—though that hardly does it justice either. His was not a simple move from Christless Judaism to Christianity. In so many ways the apostle never abandoned his Judaism. His affinity with his fellow Jews never flagged. In fact, he never ceased to feel great anxiety for the people that were his own. "I have great sorrow and unceasing anguish in my heart. For I could wish that I myself were . . . cut off from Christ for the sake of my brethren, my kinsmen by race" (Rom. 9:2, 3, RSV). He seemed to feel that when a Jew became a Christian, that person's experience was at last complete. Christianity was not a replacement for Judaism; it was the natural fulfillment of Judaism. As he works out his Christian theology, he continues to use the terms and figures of Judaism to make clear his exposition of Christianity. "He is a Jew who is one inwardly, and real circumcision is a matter of the heart, spiritual and not literal" (Rom. 2:29, RSV). Furthermore, his endless quoting of the Old Testament is further evidence that Saul's conversion was not equivalent to turning his back on Judaism in favor of Christianity. Perhaps the closest we can come to understanding Saul's conversion is to listen closely as he counseled the Romans to "be transformed by the renewal of your mind, that you may prove what is the will of God" (Rom. 12:2, RSV). Of course, the changing of one's mind is often spoken of with reference to things and ideas that can be quite superficial, even trivial. "I changed my mind; I'll take the green one instead of the red one." Conversion, on the other hand, is much more than a changing of one's mind. For that very reason Paul's "renewal of the mind" language implies something much more serious and comprehensive. A renewed mind can view life and its goals in entirely new categories, and that speaks to the transformation that completely redirected the life of our hero.

Ananias, a devoted disciple living in Damascus, was hardly thrilled to be enlisted by God to seek out Saul and explain to him the reasons behind the radical change in his travel plans. Ananias' pathos is palpable as he pleads, "Lord, I have heard from many about this man, how much evil he has done to thy saints at Jerusalem; and here he has authority from the chief priests to bind all who call upon thy name" (Acts 9:13, 14, RSV). "Could you give me a different assignment, Lord? I'd really prefer one that I could live to tell about." Saul, a man on a vendetta, would not be considered a good prospect for Bible studies. But it is a truism, forgotten by Ananias and all of us who are his godchildren, that when God gives us an assignment He will assuredly give us the resources to accomplish that assignment. If He asks us to seek out a former killer, He provides the protection and the encouragement we need to accomplish the mission. "The trial will not exceed the strength that shall be given us to bear it. . . . Whatever may come, strength proportionate to the trial will be given" (Ellen G. White, *Steps to Christ,* p. 125). At the same time, He understands our reluctance and patiently explains, again and again, that we need to trust His instructions and not our meager grasp of the situation. The directive for fearful Ananias included the encouraging and intriguing phrase "Inquire . . . for a man . . . named Saul; for behold, he is praying" (verse 11, RSV). I don't think the phrase was intended to convey the thought that Pharisees didn't pray and newborn Christians did. But the way it is said, it clearly implies that this "praying" meant that something radical had happened in Saul's life and that now the murderer is safe to approach. "Go, for he is a chosen instrument of mine to carry my name before the Gentiles and kings and the sons of Israel; for I will show him how much he must suffer for the sake of my name" (verses 15, 16, RSV). That instruction to Ananias changed everything. Not only was Saul praying, but he would soon "suffer for the sake of my name" as a consequence of taking that name to all the primary people groups throughout that part of the ancient world.

Ananias must have been shocked by what he had just heard. But apparently that shock was required to melt his skepticism and send him to knock on the door on Straight Street (verse 11). (In modern Damascus there is still a street named Straight). How completely his attitude softened is evidenced in his very first greeting to the bewildered Pharisee. "Brother Saul . . ." (verse 17). "Brother?" It must have been only a few minutes earlier that Ananias had tried to reason with the Lord to get out of this assignment completely. But the revelation that Saul was praying and that he would suffer for "the name" provided him with the necessary credentials to become a "brother." "Rabbi" was the common greeting for a leading Pharisee, as it contained just the right amount of deference and respect for the position. "Brother" had a warmer sense and came to be used commonly among the Christian community. It must have added to Saul's sense of change. Had he ever been so warmly greeted by a stranger?

When the scales fell (verse 18), and his physical and spiritual eyes were opened, he was a radically changed man. The eminent Pharisee was now a converted Christian. But, as mentioned above, that conversion was truly one of a kind. Whatever psychological preparations preceded Saul's dramatic confrontation on the road, and whatever conclusions contemporary thinkers reach about his mystical experience in Damascus, there can be little doubt that he looked back upon these events as a divine intervention that brought about the decisive change of direction in his life. Years later, when he defended himself against a mob (Acts 21:27-22:25), and again before Agrippa (Acts 26:12-18), he recounted the Damascus experience in detail, thus reflecting the awe with which he looked upon that event. He clearly viewed the experience as an act of God that had penetrated to the very core of his being and radically changed his perception. If we attempt to get more specific about just what all he was converted from and to, we will lapse into speculation, as Scripture is notably quiet about the fine details of what he was converted from and what he was converted to.

One thing is clear: his converted life was not a walk in the park. Saul could not have begun to anticipate how far-reaching would be the results. It must have sounded pretentious and more than a little ambitious to be told that your mission is to be the evangelist for the world. That assignment would prove to be merciless and never-ending. For some 30 years he had been preparing for his mission in life. But now that the time had come for him to fulfill that mission, it was suddenly and radically changed. For approximately 30 more years he would be doing the work that a nation had failed to do. That name that he had vilified and tried to stamp out he is now called to carry "before the Gentiles and kings and the sons of Israel," and that mission would be the source of what "he must suffer" (Acts 9:15, 16). As usual, the Hound of Heaven had done much more than track down the wayward. He had gotten Saul's undivided attention, convicted his conscience, commissioned him to evangelism, and sent him out to an incredible array of hostile audiences. Grace is free to all, but contrary to some popular preaching, there is always a cost to accepting heaven's invitation.

For Saul the first "cost" was coming to terms with his own past. His turnabout had been radical and genuine. At last the pieces of the puzzle all fit. But his conscience, torn and conflicted since the stoning of

Stephen, now grappled with a new problem—he was awash in guilt. How could he have been so terribly and violently wrong? Through repentance and the grace of forgiveness he would find peace, but it would always be a peace clouded by the memory of his misguided past. For example, as he reviewed for the Galatians his acceptance of God's call, the memory of his former life was still fresh and troubling. "You have heard of my former life in Judaism, how I persecuted the church of God violently and tried to destroy it" (Gal. 1:13, RSV). Still later, as he was defending himself before a crowd that wanted to kill him, his sense of shame for his past again bubbled to the surface in this prayer: "Lord, they themselves know that in every synagogue I imprisoned and beat those who believed in thee. And when the blood of Stephen thy witness was shed, I also was standing by and approving, and keeping the garments of those who killed him" (Acts 22:19, 20, RSV). It is one thing to accept God's forgiveness for sins of greed or envy; it is quite another to feel clean after sins of malicious bloodshed and murder. Perhaps that was the reason for Saul's remaining "several days . . . with the disciples at Damascus" (Acts 9:19, RSV). He needed help to somehow come to terms with all the hurt he had caused.

At length, though the memory of his past could never be completely erased, forgiveness and the freedom of the gospel finally took away his guilt. With his vision finally clear, Saul wasted no time attempting to proclaim his newfound understanding. He had been informed that his mission field would include "Gentiles and kings and the sons of Israel" (verse 15, RSV), but he seems to have reversed the order of his audiences. Perhaps he wanted to begin his mission with those he knew best, so "in the synagogues immediately he proclaimed Jesus, saying, 'He is the Son of God' " (verse 20, RSV). But just as "immediately" he experienced the reverse of open arms. In fact, he suddenly realized that the hunter had become the hunted. "When many days had passed, the Jews plotted to kill him" (verse 23, RSV). He had come to Damascus "breathing threats and murder against the disciples of the Lord" (verse 1, RSV). He left town with others breathing those very threats against him. The tables had taken quite a turn.

Then began what must have been one of the most disturbing, frustrating periods in the apostle's life. For the first time in his life he had the full story about Jesus straight, and, given his personal makeup, he was itching to get the message out—he had to share his newly discovered good news. The trouble was that he had no receptive audience. His fellow Jews saw him as a traitor and wanted him dead. The earliest Christians had memories too, and they were sure he was a wolf in sheep's clothing. They didn't want to kill him, but they certainly wanted to keep him at arm's length. No doubt Ananias had spoken for them all when he said, "Lord, I have heard from many about this man, how much evil he has done to thy saints" (verse 13, RSV). No, the other apostles needed more time and evidence before they could trust him. So where could he go to proclaim his exciting new discovery? The Messiah, the message, and the mission were now all crystal clear in his mind, but no one would believe that his enthusiastic delivery was genuine. For such an active, excited man, his frustration must have gripped him like a vise. Where was his audience? Where could he proclaim his story? He had to do something, but what? Why was no mission field open? He had been called an evangelist for all people, except no group would give him anything close to a sympathetic ear. The Christians distrusted him, the Gentiles would scoff at him, and the Jews—well, they were willing to listen to him, but only because they hoped to find something in his words upon which they could arrest him, try him, and then have him killed. Ananias had promised Saul that he was to go to all these people groups, but he had, in that context, also warned him "how much he must suffer for the sake of my name" (verse 16, RSV). Mentally and emotionally the suffering was already beginning. Little did he know that the physical suffering would come later and would also be intense. As his frustration grew, Saul felt the need to get away to some quiet place where he could sort it all out. "I did not confer with flesh and blood, nor did I go up to Jerusalem to those who were apostles before me, but I went away into Arabia. . . . Then after three years I went up to Jerusalem" (Gal. 1:16-18, RSV).

At this point in his life Saul was experiencing what we find it hard, if not embarrassing, to talk about—that is, how frequently life after conversion becomes more difficult than it was before. We are so benefit-conscious; we want assurances that any significant change in our lives that costs will bring us some reward or dividend. Such a view has given rise to a philosophy that cuts across many denominations: accept Christ, and the hard questions will all be answered; pay tithe, and your financial picture will improve; accept the King, and you will be able to tap into His wealth; if you lose your job because of your religion, you'll get a better job; accepting Christ is not a sacrifice when you think of the reward: "Happiness is the Lord." That kind of gospel sells well. We are not very inclined to include in our evangelistic appeals a statement that to give our lives to Him will almost certainly mean that suffering will eventually follow. In any case, Saul's conversion thrust him into a life of suffering from which only his death would ultimately free him. Saul's situation is instructive for the person who, at great sacrifice, has managed to complete a college education, only to find no job. I have felt the anxiety and hurt as theology graduates have wondered aloud why God would impress them to leave a secure job, move the family away from friends and comfortable circumstances, take out loans, train for the ministry, and then not impress any conference to hire them.

There is the feeling of resignation in the phrase "I went away into Arabia." It is one thing to respond to Heaven's Hound and turn your face toward God. But from that point to the place where He destined us to work for Him can be a protracted testing of our newfound faith. Perhaps our first love experience needs a time of gradual toughening before it will be ready to bear the test of perseverance. For the converted Paul it would be several years before he would find his niche and the term *apostle* ("sent one") would really fit him. After the mysteriously silent three years in Arabia, his role as Christian evangelist was still further delayed. While the chronology of events is less than clear, there is reason to believe that Paul's Galatians 1:17 reference to his Arabian sojourn should be inserted into the Acts record somewhere between the account of his conversion and his return to Jerusalem (Acts 9:18, 19; Gal. 1:17; Acts 9:28). But his visit to Jerusalem was rocky, because when "he attempted to join the disciples . . . they were all afraid of him, for they did not believe that he was a disciple" (Acts 9:26, RSV). The visit ended when "they brought him down to Caesarea, and sent him off to Tarsus" (verse 30, RSV). More time went by, during which that commission by Ananias about his role as evangelist to the "Gentiles and kings and the sons of Israel" must have had an increasingly hollow ring to it. In time, however, he would come to acknowledge that while the shaping of his life had taken some 30 years, the reshaping took several more. The making of Paul the evangelist meant the unmaking of Saul the Pharisee. Only God knows when the molding of our lives has reached that place where we are finally fitted for fulfilling His mission.

In time the need for evangelistic help in the infant Christian community became critical, so Barnabas went to Tarsus looking for Saul. In the wisdom and planning of God the time was now right for both the apostle and the church, so the now completely molded Paul accompanied Barnabas back to Antioch, which had become the real center for Christian outreach (Acts 11:26). There in Antioch, a short time later, "the Holy Spirit said, 'Set apart for me Barnabas and Saul for the work to which I have called them' " (Acts 13:2, RSV). Over a trying and torturous trail, the apostle had reached his destiny. Like Moses of old, Saul had received an excellent formal education. Also like Moses, he had now spent some time in the wilderness being reeducated for his real mission. Thanks to his thorough and protracted preparation he would never look back, though he would often have reason to. His time as trainee had tested his patience; his life as apostle would test his mettle. "Five times I have received . . . forty lashes less one. Three times I have been beaten with rods; once I was stoned. Three times I have been shipwrecked; a night and a day I have been adrift at sea; on frequent journeys, in danger from rivers, danger from robbers, danger from my own people, danger from Gentiles, danger in the city, danger in the wilderness, danger at sea, danger from false brethren; in toil and hardship, through many a sleepless night, in hunger and thirst, often without food, in cold and exposure. And, apart from other things, there is the daily pressure upon me of my anxiety for all the churches" (2 Cor. 11:25-28, RSV). Paul's case was extreme, but the lesson to be learned is broad—when the Hound of Heaven calls us back, the cost will be significant.